My Favorite Quotes

Ability

to Youth

By

Pardu S. Ponnapalli, Ph.D.

Dedicated to

My son-

My fondest wish is to have more time with you as you grow up

Table of Contents

Preface to the Second Edition

Over the years, I have developed a collection of favorite quotations related to a wide variety of topics. The quotations I enjoy the most are ones that remind me of a life event or my own experiences. Sometimes they remind me of the experiences of close friends I had. The power of quotations is that they summarize the essence of life in a short and concise manner. I find that very refreshing especially in this day and age where everyone has a publicist to explain their ideas and make them palatable to the public. There is something essentially honest and truthful in quotations. You could probably find one quotation to explain most of the political speeches that abound and you could save a lot of time by reading it and not the long speech.

There is also the aspect that many of them provoke thought and a different way of looking at the world. The economy of doing that without having to read dozens of books on philosophy is also very attractive. One is expected to think through the implications by the planting of an idea in a pithy way, instead of lengthier expositions that try to feed your mind and not spark your imagination. In the world of quotations all is clear and simple, yet complex and thought provoking at the same time. The resonance of these quotes for me lies in their reminder of my experiences in life and those of my friends, acquaintances and passing conversations with strangers. This book is available in two different formats. This version is a consolidation of 18 individual volumes, all of which are available in the Kindle store.

 I hope this book provides some enjoyable time away from the vicissitudes of day to day life. The topics covered are "Art" to "Youth" as is evident from the Table of Contents. All the topics are arranged in lexicographic order in the various volumes.

For the second edition, I corrected several typographical errors and streamlined the formatting.

April 18, 2017

Chapter 1 Ability

"Ability is nothing without opportunity."   Napoleon Bonaparte

"Don't measure yourself by what you have accomplished, but by what you should have accomplished with your ability." John Wooden

"Ability is what you're capable of doing. Motivation determines what you do. Attitude determines how well you do it." Raymond Chandler

"There is something that is much more scarce, something rarer than ability. It is the ability to recognize ability" Robert Half

"I do the very best I know how- the very best I can; and I mean to keep doing so until the end. If the end brings me out allright, what is said against me won't amount to anything. If the end brings me out wrong, ten angels swearing I was right would make no difference." Abraham Lincoln

"Behind every able man there are always other able men." Chinese Proverb

"We are not in a position in which we have nothing to work with. We already have capacities, talents, missions, directions, callings." Abraham Maslo

"Never tell a young person that anything cannot be done. God may have been waiting centuries for someone ignorant enough of the impossible to do that very thing." John Andrew Holmes

"Ability is a poor mans's wealth." John Wooden

"I know of no more encouraging fact than the unquestioned ability of man to elevate his life by conscious endeavor." Henry David Thoreau

"I sometimes think that God in creating man, somewhat overestimated his ability." Oscar Wilde

Chapter 2 Acting

"The thing about performance, even if it's only an illusion is that it is a celebration of the fact that we do contain within ourselves infinite possibilities." Daniel Day Lewis

" Acting provides the fulfillment of never being fulfilled. You're never as good as you'd like to be. So there's always something to hope for." Washington Irving

"Acting is nothing more or less than playing. The idea is to humanize lift." George Eliot " I think that acting satisfied the need and desire for approval." William Shatner

" Acting has given me a way to channel my angst. I feel like an overweight pimply faced kid a lot of time- and finding a way to access that insecurity, and put it toward something creative is incredibly rewarding. I feel very lucky." Ryan Reynolds

" Your performance is not about you. It is about giving the gift of your talents to your audience." Marianni Magnuson

"The actor should be able to create the universe in the palm of his hand." Laurence Olivier

"I love acting but I don't like the other stuff associated with it. The interest in celebrities, the press, the Internet, when your identify becomes mixed up in the way people are perceiving you." Nicole Kidman

"Bad acting is the ultimate inconsideration." Debra Winger

"I do find acting cathartic." Francesca Annis

Chapter 3 Adversity

"Adversity has ever been considered the state in which a man most easily becomes acquainted with himself." Samuel Johnson

"All the adversity I've had in my life, all my troubles and obstacles, have strengthened me... You may not realize it when it happens, but a kick in the teeth may be the best thing in the world for you." Walt Disney

"Adversity causes some men to break; others to break records." William Arthur Ward

"In times of great stress or adversity, it's always best to keep busy, to plow your anger and your energy into something positive" Lee Iacocca

"Adversity reveals genius, prosperity conceals it."   Horace

"Always seek out the seed of triumph in every adversity." Og Mandino

"You'll never find a better sparring partner than adversity." Golda Meir

"He knows not his own strength that hath not met adversity." Cesare Pavese

"Nearly all men can stand adversity, but if you want to test a man's character, give him power." Abraham Lincoln

"However mean your life is, meet it and live it." Henry David Thoreau

Chapter 4 Advertising

"Many a small thing has been made large by the right kind of advertising." Mark Twain

"Advertising may be described as the science of arresting human intelligence long enough to get money from it." Stephen Leacock

"Advertising is totally unnecessary. Unless you hope to make money." Jef I. Richard

"The average TV commercial of sixty seconds has one hundred and twenty half-second clips in it, or one-third of a second. We bombard people with sensation. That substitutes for thinking." Ray Bradbury

"Advertising is fundamentally persuasion and persuasion happens to be not a science, but an art." William Bernbach

"If I were starting life over again, I am inclined to think that I would go into the advertising business in preference to almost any other. The general raising of standards of modern civilization among all groups of people during the past half century would have been impossible without spreading the knowledge of higher standards by means of advertising." Franklin D. Roosevelt

"Advertising is the modern substitute for argument; its function is to make the worse appear the better." George Santanaya

"What you say in advertisting is more important than how you say it." David Ogilvy

"First we thought the PC was a calculator. Then we found out how to turn numbers into letters with ASCII- and we thought it was a typewriter. Then we discovered graphics, and we thought it was a

television. With the World Wide Web, we've realized it's a brochure."
Douglas Adams

Chapter 5 Advice

"Advice is like castor oil, easy enough to give but dreadful uneasy to take." Josh Billings

"When we ask for advice, we are usually looking for an accomplice." Saul Bellow

"If it's free, it's advice; if you pay for it, it's counseling; if you can use either one, it's a miracle." Jack Adams

"A leader must have the courage to act against an expert's advice." James Callaghan

"An expert is somebody who is more than 50 miles from home, has no responsibility for implementing the advice he gives, and shows slides." Edwin Meese

"Men give away nothing so liberally as their advice" Francois de La Rochefoucauld

"My advice is: if you've got to be miserable to write great music, then drive a truck." Chris Isaak

"In real life, the most practical advice for leaders is not to treat pawns like pawns, nor princes like princes, but all persons like persons." James MacGregor Burns

"The true secret of giving advice is, after you have honestly given it, to be perfectly indifferent whether it is taken or not, and never persist in trying to set people right" Hannah Whitall Smith

"Many receive advice, few profit by it."   Publilius Syrus Autu

"We cling to our own point of view, as though everything depended on it. Yet our opinions have no permanence; like autumn and winter, they gradually pass away." Zhuangzi

Chapter 6 Age

"Beware of the young doctor and the old barber." Benjamin Franklin

"I was always taught to respect my elders and I've now reached the age when I don't have anybody to respect." George Burns

"The first half of life consists of the capacity to enjoy without the chance; the last half consists of the chance withouth the capacity" Mark Twain

"It is a mistake to regard age as a downhill grade toward dissolution. The reverse is true. As one grows older, one climbs with surprising strides." George Sand

"Some day you will be old enough to start reading fairy tales again." C.S. Lewis

"There is a fountain of youth: it is your mind, your talents, the creativity you bring to your life and the lives of people you love. When you learn to tap this source, you will truly have defeated age." Sophia Loren

"The error of youth is to believe that intelligence is a substitute for experience, while the error of age is to believe experience is a substitute for intelligence." Lyman Bryson

"The aging process has you firmly in its grasp if you never get the urge to throw a snowball."   Doug Larson

"Old age isn't so bad when you consider the alternatives." Maurice Chevalier

"The older I get the better I used to be!" Lee Trevino

Chapter 7 Agreement

"My idea of an agreeable person is a person who agrees with me."
Benjamin Disraeli

"If you can find something everyone agrees on, it's wrong." Mo Udall

"My people and I have come to an agreement which satisfied us both. They are to say what they please, and I am to do what I please." Frederick the Great

"Make fair agreements and stick to them." Confucius

"You can get assent to almost any proposition so long as you are not going to do anything about it." John Jay Chapman

"Meetings are a great trap. Soon you find yourself trying to get agreement and then the people who disagree come to think they have a right to be persuaded. However, they are indispensable when you don't want to do anything." John Kenneth Galbraith

"He that complies against his will is of his own opinion still." Samuel Butler

"You may easily play a joke on a man who likes to argue -- agree with him." Edward W. Howard

Chapter 8 Ambition

**"I had a family, I had children, I got married. My ambition changed."
Penelope Ann Miller**

"A man without ambition is dead. A man with ambition but no love is dead. A man with ambition and love for his blessings here on earth is ever so alive. Having been alive, it won't be so hard in the end to lie down and rest." Pearl Bailey

"Keep away from people who try to belittle your ambitions. Small people always do that, but the really great make you feel that you , too, can become great." Mark Twain

"Dreams, goals, ambitions- these are the stuff man uses for fuel." L Ron Hubbard

"Few are more unhappy than those who have great ambition, but little energy to urge it into activity." Norman McDonald

"Nothing can stop the man with the right mental attitude from achieving his goal; nothing on earth can help the man with the wrong mental attitude." Thomas Jefferson

"Ambition has one heel nailed in well, though she stretch her fingers to touch the heavens." Lao Tzu

"I had no ambition to make a fortune. Mere money-making has never been my goal. I had an ambition to build." John D. Rockefeller

"When you are aspiring to the highest place, it is honorable to reach the second or even third rank." Cicero

"Intelligence without ambition is a bird without wings." C. Archie Danielson

Chapter 9 Anger

"Speak when you are angry – and you will make the best speech you'll ever regret." Laurence J. Peter

"When anger rises, think of the consequences." Confucius

"For every minute you are angry you lose sixty seconds of happiness." Ralph Waldo Emerson

"Anger is never without a reason, but seldom with a good one." Benjamin Franklin

"In a controversy, the instant we feel anger, we have already ceased striving for truth and begun striving for ourselves." Abraham J. Heschel

"There are two things a person should never be angry at, what they can help, and what they cannot." Plato

"It is wise to direct your anger towards problems – not people; to focus your energies on answers – not excuses." William Arthur Ward

"Anger is a great force. If you control it, it can be transmuted into a power which can move the whole world." William Shenstone

"When a man sends you an impudent letter, sit right down and give it back to him with interest ten times compounded, and then throw both letters in the wastebasket." Elbert Hubbard

"The sharpest sword is a word spoken in wrath." Buddha

Chapter 10 Argument

"In a heated argument we are apt to lose sight of the truth." Publilius Syrus

"It is senseless to argue with someone whose sole purpose in life is not to be convinced of anything." Jon Campbell

"Ridicule is the first and last argument of a fool." Charles Simmons

"No matter what side of an argument you are on, you always find people on your side that you wish were on the other." Thomas Berger

"When you let someone else win an argument, often you both end up winners." Richard Carlson

"Argument is the worst sort of conversation." Jonathan Swift

"It is not necessary to understand things in order to argue about them." Pierre Augustin de Beaumarchais

"Discussion is an exchange of information, argument is an exchange of ignorance." Robert Quillen

"Strong and bitter words indicate a weak cause." Victor Hugo

Chapter 11 Art

"The purpose of art is washing the dust of daily life off our souls."
Pablo Picasso

"A man paints with his brains and not with his hands." Michelangelo

"This world is but a canvas to our imagination."   Henry David Thoreau

"All art is but imitation of nature." Lucius Annaeus Seneca

"Painting, n.: The art of protecting flat surfaces from the weather, and exposing them to the critic." Ambrose Bierce

"Art is a collaboration between God and the artist, and the less the artist does the better." Andre Gide

"Art is born of the observation and investigation of nature." Cicero

"Without art the crudeness of reality would make the world unbearable." George Bernard Shaw

"Every artist dips his brush in his own soul, and paints his own nature into his pictures." Henry Ward Beecher

"Life beats down and crushes the soul and art reminds you that you have one."   Stella Adler

Chapter 12 Atheism

"Atheism is a non-prophet organization." George Carlin

"The very idea of carrying my memory into eternity devastated me, and I took refuge in atheism." Taylor Caldwell

"If there is a God, atheism must seem to Him as less of an insult than religion." Edmond de Goncourt

"We must question the story logic of having an all-knowing all-powerful God, who creates faulty Humans, and then blames them for his own mistakes. " Gene Roddenberry

"I still say a church steeple with a lightning rod on top shows a lack of confidence." Doug McLeod

"We must respect the other fellow's religion, but only in the sense and to the extent that we respect his theory that his wife is beautiful and his children smart." H. L. Mencken

"Which is it, is man one of God's blunders or is God one of man's?" Friedrich Nietzsche

"Most people can`t bear to sit in church for an hour on Sundays. How are they supposed to live somewhere very similar to it for eternity?" Mark Twain

"Most people can't bear to sit in church for an hour on Sundays. How are they supposed to live somewhere to it for eternity?" Mark Twain

"I am against religion because it teaches us to be satisfied with not understanding the world." Richard Dawkins

"The power of god has given men the ability to realize that he does not exist." Andre dos Santos

Chapter 13 Attitude

"Weakness of attitude becomes weakness of character." Albert Einstein

"Your attitude, not your aptitude, will determine your altitude." Zig Ziglar

"A positive attitude is not going to save you. What it's going to do is, every day, between now and the day you die, whether that's a short time from now or a long time from now, that every day, you're going to actually live." Elizabeth Edwards

"Our spiritual attitude is determined by our conception of our relation to infinite spirit." Paul Twitchell

"An attitude of philosophic doubt, of suspended judgment, is repugnant to the natural man. Belief is an independent joy to him." William Minto

"Everyone thinks of changing the world, but no one thinks of changing himself." Leo Tolstoy

"In one minute you can change your attitude and in that minute you can change your entire day." Spencer Johnson

"Whenever you're in conflict with someone, there is one factor that can make the difference between damaging your relationship and deepening it. That factor is attitude." William James

"Attitude is more important than the past, than education, than money, than circumstances, than what people do or say. It is more important than appearance, giftedness, or skill." W.C Fields

"If you can't change your fate, change your attitude." Amy Tan

Chapter 14 Authority

"Do not believe in anything simply because you have heard it. Do not believe in anything simply because it is spoken and rumored by many. Do not believe in anything simply because it is found written in your religious books. Do not believe in anything merely on the authority of your teachers and elders. Do not believe in traditions because they have been handed down for many generations. But after observation and analysis, when you find that anything agrees with reason and is conducive to the good and benefit of one and all, then accept it and live up to it." The Buddha

"To punish me for my contempt for authority, fate made me an authority myself." Albert Einstein

"Whoever in discussion adduces authority uses not intellect but memory." Leonardo da Vinci

"Leave no authority existing not responsible to the people." Thomas Jefferson

"Think for yourself and question authority." Timothy Leary

"Every great advance in natural knowledge has involved the absolute rejection of authority." Thomas Huxley

"My desire to devolve authority has nothing to do with a wish to shirk responsibility." Dalai Lama

"The people are hungry: It is because those in authority eat up too much in taxes." Lao Tzu

"In order to be respected, authority has got to be respectable." Tom Robbins

"The key to successful leadership today is influence, not authority." Ken Blanchard

Chapter 15 Autumn

"Autumn is a second spring when every leaf is a flower." Albert Camus

"We cling to our own point of view, as though everything depended on it. Yet our opinions have no permanence; like autumn and winter, they gradually pass away." Zhuangzi

"Fall is my favorite season in Los Angeles, watching the birds change color and fall from the trees." David Letterman

"Autumn, the year's last, loveliest smile." William Cullen Bryant

"Every leaf speaks bliss to me, fluttering from the autumn tree." Emily Bronte

"Delicious autumn! My very soul is wedded to it, and if I were a bird I would fly about the earth seeking the successive autumns." George Eliot

"Autumn is the eternal corrective. It is ripeness and color and a time of maturity; but it is also breadth, and depth, and distance. What man can stand with autumn on a hilltop and fail to see the span of his world and the meaning of the rolling hills that reach to the far horizon?" Hal Borland

"Nothing is more fleeting than external form, which withers and alters like the flowers of the field at the appearance of autumn." Umberto Eco

"Summer is already better, but the best is autumn. It is mature, reasonable and serious, it glows moderately and not frivolously... It cools down, clears up, makes you reasonable..." Valentin

"Change is a measure of time and, in the autumn, time seems speeded up. What was is not and never again will be; what is is change." Edwin Teale

"Our judgment ripens; our imagination decays. We cannot at once enjoy the flowers of the Spring of life and the fruits of its Autumn." Thomas Macaulay

Chapter 16 Balance

"Life is like riding a bicycle. To keep your balance you must keep moving" Albert Einstein

"A well-developed sense of humor is the pole that adds balance to your steps as you walk the tightrope of life." William Arthur Ward

"The best and safest thing is to keep a balance in your life, acknowledge the great powers around us and in us. If you can do that, and live that way, you are really a wise man." Euripides

"As we look deeply within, we understand our perfect balance. There is no fear of the cycle of birth, life and death. For when you stand in the present moment, you are timeless." Rodney Yee

"Fortunate indeed, is the man who takes exactly the right measure of himself, and holds a just balance between what he can acquire and what he can use." Peter Mere Latham

"So divinely is the world organized that every one of us, in our place and time, is in balance with everything else." Johann Wolfgang von Goethe

"Be aware of wonder. Live a balanced life - learn some and think some and draw and paint and sing and dance and play and work every day some." Robert Fulghum

"Man always travels along precipices. His truest obligation is to keep his balance." Pope John Paul II

"What I dream of is an art of balance." Henri Matisse

"Something in human nature causes us to start slacking off at our moment of greatest accomplishment. As you become successful, you will need a great deal of self-discipline not to lose your sense of balance, humility, and commitment." H. Ross Perot

Chapter 17 Banks

"A bank is a place that will lend you money if you can prove that you don't need it." Bob Hope

"I believe that banking institutions are more dangerous to our liberties than standing armies. If the American people ever allow private banks to control the issue of their currency, first by inflation, then by deflation, the banks and corporations that will grow up around [the banks] will deprive the people of all property until their children wake-up homeless on the continent their fathers conquered. The issuing power should be taken from the banks and restored to the people, to whom it properly belongs." Thomas Jefferson

"A banker is a fellow who lends you his umbrella when the sun is shining, but wants it back the minute it begins to rain." Mark Twain

"I have always been afraid of banks." Andrew Jackson

"But if you want to continue to be slaves of the banks and pay the cost of your own slavery, then let bankers continue to create money and control credit." Josiah Stamp

"I am afraid that the ordinary citizen will not like to be told that the banks can and do create and destroy money. And they who control the credit of a nation direct the policy of governments, and hold in the hollow of their hands the destiny of the people." Richard McKenna

"Investment banking has, in recent years, resembled a casino, and the massive scale of gambling losses has dragged down traditional business and retail lending activities as banks try to rebuild their balance sheets. This was one aspect of modern financial liberalisation that had dire consequences." Vince Cable

"Good bankers, like good tea, can only be appreciated when they are in hot water." Jaffar Hussein

"With a group of bankers I always had the feeling that success was measured by the extent one gave nothing away." Lord Longford

"It is well enough that people of the nation do not understand our banking and monetary system, for if they did, I believe there would be a revolution before tomorrow morning." Henry Ford

Chapter 18 Beauty

"Beauty is only temporary, but your mind lasts you a lifetime." Alicia Machado

"Beauty, to me, is about being comfortable in your own skin. That, or a kick-ass red lipstick." Gwyneth Paltrow

"Beauty is a short-lived tyranny." George Bernard Shaw

"Beauty is less important than quality." Eugene Ormandy

"Love built on beauty, soon as beauty, dies." John Donne

"Beauty is the first present nature gives to women and the first it takes away." Fay Weldon

"Beauty is that which is simultaneously attractive and sublime." Karl Wilhelm Friedrich

"Beauty is whatever gives joy." Edna St. Vincent Millay

"Most women are dissatisfied with their appearance - it's the stuff that fuels the beauty and fashion industries." Annie Lennox

"Beauty is not just physical." Halle Berry

Chapter 19 Belief

"Men willingly believe what they wish." Julius Caesar

"I would never die for my beliefs because I might be wrong." Bertrand Russell

"The fact that a believer is happier than a skeptic is no more to the point than the fact that a drunken man is happier than a sober one." George Bernard Shaw

"I would rather have a mind opened by wonder than one closed by belief." Gerry Spence

"Every man prefers belief to the exercise of judgment." Lucius Annaeus Seneca

"Against my will, in the course of my travels, the belief that everything worth knowing was known at Cambridge gradually wore off. In this respect my travels were very useful to me." Bertrand Russell

"If some people have the belief or view that the Dalai Lama has some miracle power, that's totally nonsense." Dalai Lama

"Most executives, many scientists, and almost all business school graduates believe that if you analyze data, this will give you new ideas. Unfortunately, this belief is totally wrong. The mind can only see what it is prepared to see." Edward de Bono

"There is no greater level and form of belief than believing in yourself." Darren L. Johnson

"A belief which leaves no place for doubt is not a belief; it is a superstition." Jose Bergamin

Chapter 20 Birds

"A bird does not sing because it has an answer. It sings because it has a song." Chinese Proverb

"You cannot fly like an eagle with the wings of a wren." William Henry Hudson

"No bird soars too high if he soars with his own wings." William Blake

"Everyone likes birds. What wild creature is more accessible to our eyes and ears, as close to us and everyone in the world, as universal as a bird?" David Attenborough

"I realized that If I had to choose, I would rather have birds than airplanes." Charles Lindbergh

"Caged birds accept each other but flight is what they long for." Tennessee Williams

"Birds sing after a storm; why shouldn't people feel as free to delight in whatever sunlight remains to them?" Rose Kennedy

"A wise old owl sat on an oak; The more he saw the less he spoke; The less he spoke the more he heard; Why aren't we like that wise old bird?" Edward Hersey Richards

" God loved the birds and invented trees. Man loved the birds and invented cages." Jacques Deval

"Much talking is the cause of danger. Silence is the means of avoiding misfortune. The talkative parrot is shut up in a cage. Other birds, without speech, fly freely about." Saskya Pandita

Chapter 21 Birth

"Some people are born on third base and go through life thinking they hit a triple." Barry Switzer

"There is no cure for birth and death save to enjoy the interval." George Santayana

"A man is great by deeds, not by birth." Chanakya

"After your death you will be what you were before your birth." Arthur Schopenhauer

"Man has but three events in his life: to be born, to live, and to die. He is not conscious of his birth, he suffers at his death and he forgets to live." Jean de la Bruyere

"Adolescence is a new birth, for the higher and more completely human traits are now born." G. Stanley Hall

"Life is like a very short visit to a toyshop between birth and death." Desmond Morris

"There should be weeping at a man's birth, not at his death." Charles Louis de Secondat Montesquieu

"Birth and death are not two different states, but they are different aspects of the same state. There is as little reason to deplore the one as there is to be pleased over the other." Mahatma Gandhi

"Birth is the sudden opening of a window, through which you look out upon a stupendous prospect. For what has happened? A miracle. You have exchanged nothing for the possibility of everything." William MacNeile Dixon

Chapter 22 Body

"Be sure that it is not you that is mortal, but only your body. For that man whom your outward form reveals is not yourself; the spirit is the true self, not that physical figure which and be pointed out by your finger." Cicero

"Our bodies communicate to us clearly and specifically, if we are willing to listen to them." Shakti Gawain

"Our bodies are our gardens to which our wills are gardeners." William Shakespeare

"Take care of your body. It's the only place you have to live." Jim Rohn

"After thirty, a body has a mind of its own." Bette Midler

"It is not the end of the physical body that should worry us. Rather, our concern must be to live while we're alive - to release our inner selves from the spiritual death that comes with living behind a facade designed to conform to external definitions of who and what we are." Elisabeth Kubler-Ross

"Age wrinkles the body. Quitting wrinkles the soul." Douglas MacArthur

"The best cure for the body is a quiet mind." Napoleon Bonaparte

"No diet will remove all the fat from your body because the brain is entirely fat. Without a brain, you might look good, but all you could do is run for public office." George Bernard Shaw

"Begin to see yourself as a soul with a body rather than a body with a soul." Wayne Dyer

Chapter 23 Books

"A room without books is like a body without a soul." Cicero

"Resolve to edge in a little reading every day, if it is but a single sentence. If you gain fifteen minutes a day, it will make itself felt at the end of the year." Horace Mann

"A good book is enjoyable. A great book sets off a bomb inside of you." Ned Hepburn

"In the highest civilization, the book is still the highest delight. He who has once known its satisfactions is provided with a resource against calamity."   Ralph Waldo Emerson

"When I step into this library, I cannot understand why I ever step out of it." Marie de Sevigne

"Read not to contradict and confute, nor to find talk and discourse, but to weigh and consider." Sir Francis Bacon

"When I read a book I seem to read it with my eyes only, but now and then I come across a passage, perhaps only a phrase, which has a meaning for me, and it becomes part of me." W. Somerset Maugham

"A good book should leave you... slightly exhausted at the end. You live several lives while reading it." William Styron

" A book is like a garden carried in the pocket."   Chinese Proverb

" Books are embalmed minds."   Bovee

Chapter 24 Boredom

"Work spares us from three evils: boredom, vice, and need" Voltaire

"The cure for boredom is curiosity. There is no cure for curiosity."
Ellen Parr

 "The word aerobics comes from two Greek words: aero, meaning
"ability to," and bics, meaning "withstand tremendous boredom"."
Dave Barry

 "I don't believe in an afterlife, so I don't have to spend my whole life
fearing hell, or fearing heaven even more. For whatever the tortures of
hell, I think the boredom of heaven would be even worse." Isaac
Asimov

"Virtuous people often revenge themselves for the constraints to which
they submit by the boredom which they inspire." Confucious

"Grasp your opportunities, no matter how poor your health; nothing is
worse for your health than boredom." Mignon McLaughlin

 "Nobody is bored when he is trying to make something that is
beautiful, or to discover something that is true." William Inge

 "Life is as tedious as a twice-told tale Vexing the dull ear of a drowsy
man." William Shakespeare

 "Against boredom the gods themselves fight in vain." Friedrich
Nietzsche

 "Want and boredom are indeed the twin poles of human life." Arthur
Schopenhauer

Chapter 25 Brain

"What a splendid head, yet no brain." Aesop

"Brain: an apparatus with which we think we think." Ambrose Bierce

"The brain is a wonderful organ. It starts working the moment you get up in the morning and does not stop until you get into the office." Robert Frost

"Any man who reads too much and uses his own brain too little falls into lazy habits of thinking." Albert Einstein

"An idea not coupled with action will never get any bigger than the brain cell it occupied." Arnold H. Glasow

"I have always had this view about the modern education system: we pay attention to brain development, but the development of warmheartedness we take for granted." Dalai Lama

"There is a real danger that computers will develop intelligence and take over. We urgently need to develop direct connections to the brain so that computers can add to human intelligence rather than be in opposition." Stephen Hawking

"One way to compensate for a tiny brain is to pretend to be dead." Scott Adams

"Humor is by far the most significant activity of the human brain." Edward de Bono

"Science Fiction will never run out of things to wonder about until the human race ceases to use its brain." Julian May

Chapter 26 Bureaucracy

"Every revolution evaporates and leaves behind only the slime of a new bureaucracy." Franz Kafka

"Bureaucracy defends the status quo long past the time when the quo has lost its status." Laurence J. Peter

"Bureaucracy is the death of all sound work" Albert Einstein

"Most managers were trained to be the thing they most despise -- bureaucrats." Alvin Toffler

"Bureaucracy, the rule of no one, has become the modern form of despotism" Mary McCarthy

"The perfect bureaucrat everywhere is the man who manages to make no decisions and escape all responsibility." Brooks Atkinson

"Any sufficiently advanced bureaucracy is indistinguishable from molasses." Unknown

"Hell hath no fury like a bureaucrat scorned." Milton Friedman

"The disease which inflicts bureaucracy and what they usually die from is routine." John Stuart Mill

"There is something about a bureaucrat that does not like a poem." Gore Vidal

Chapter 27 Business

"All lasting business is built on friendship." Alfred A. Montapert

"There is only one boss. The customer. And he can fire everybody in the company from the chairman on down, simply by spending his money somewhere else." Sam Walton

"Business is never so healthy as when, like a chicken, it must do a certain amount of scratching around for what it gets." Henry Ford

"Business is a combination of war and sport." Andre Maurois

"If you don't drive your business, you will be driven out of business." B. C. Forbes

"A dinner lubricates business." Lord William Stowell

"In the business world, the rearview mirror is always clearer than the windshield." Warren Buffett

"In the business world, everyone is paid in two coins: cash and experience.   Take the experience first; the cash will come later." Harold Geneen

Chapter 28 Camping

"Camping is nature's way of promoting the motel business." Dave Barry

"Kneeling over a trickling mountain stream and pumping every ounce of water you use though a filter can really change your perception of turning on a faucet." Eric Voorhis

"People say to me so often, 'Jane how can you be so peaceful when everywhere around you people want books signed, people are asking these questions and yet you seem peaceful,' and I always answer that it is the peace of the forest that I carry inside." Jane Goodall

"Keep close to Nature's heart... and break clear away, once in awhile, and climb a mountain or spend a week in the woods. Wash your spirit clean. None of Nature's landscapes are ugly so long as they are wild." John Muir

"Some national parks have long waiting lists for camping reservations. When you have to wait a year to sleep next to a tree, something is wrong." George Carlin

"Campers: Nature's way of feeding mosquitoes." Author Unknown

"Live in the sunshine, swim the sea, drink the wild air." Ralph Waldo Emerson

"Seeing wildlife is like seeing celebrities, only better." Tanja Andrews

"The wild life of today is not ours to do with as we please. The original stock was given to us in trust for the benefit both of the present and the future. We must render an accounting of this trust to those who come after us." Theodore Roosevelt

"There is a solitude, or perhaps a solemnity, in the few hours that precede the dawn of day which is unlike that of any others in the twenty-four, and which I cannot explain or account for. Thoughts come to me at this time that I never have at any other." George Bird Grinnel

"Each evening, I ached for the shelter of my tent, for the smallest sense that something was shielding me from the entire rest of the world, keeping me safe not from danger, but from vastness itself. I loved the dim, clammy dark of my tent, the cozy familiarity of the way I arranged my few belongings all around me each night." Cheryl Strayed

Chapter 29 Cats

"No matter how much cats fight, there always seems to be plenty of kittens." Abraham Lincoln

"I have studied many philosophers and many cats. The wisdom of cats is infinitely superior." Hippolyte Taine

"After scolding one's cat one looks into its face and is seized by the ugly suspicion that it understood every word. And has filed it for reference." Charlotte Gray

"Thousands of years ago, cats were worshipped as gods. Cats have never forgotten this." Anonymous

"A cat sees no good reason why it should obey another animal, even if it does stand on two legs." Sarah Thompson

"Dogs come when they're called; cats take a message and get back to you later." Mary Bly

"When I play with my cat, who knows if I am not a pastime to her more than she is to me?" Montaigne

"Cats are the ultimate narcissists. You can tell this by all the time they spend on personal grooming. Dogs aren't like this. A dog's idea of personal grooming is to roll in a dead fish." James Gorman

"As every cat owner knows, nobody owns a cat." Ellen Perry Berkeley

"The phrase "domestic cat" is an oxymoron." George F. Will

Chapter 30 Celebrities

"Actors didn't use to be celebrities. A hundred years ago, they put the theaters next to the brothels." Joseph Gordon-Levitt

"Time makes heroes but dissolves celebrities." Daniel J. Boorstin

"I am utterly bored by celebrity interviews. Most celebrities are devoid of interest." Roger Ebert

"People think celebrities don't have to worry about human things like sickness and death and rent. It's like you've traveled to this Land of Celebrity, this other country. They want you to tell about what you saw." David Duchovny

"I developed a deep sadness for celebrities, a pity that they often are caught in a plastic world that runs too hard and too fast, and that many times that world means destroyed relationships with everyone they know and love." Karen Kingsbury

"Celebrities say the darnedest things." Bridgette Wilson

"A sign of celebrity is that his name is often worth more than his services." Daniel J. Boorstin

"The nice thing about being a celebrity is that when you bore people, they think it's their fault." Henry Kissinger

"When once a man has made celebrity necessary to his happiness, he has put it in the power of the weakest and most timorous malignity, if not to take away his satisfaction, at least to withhold it. His enemies may indulge their pride by airy negligence and gratify their malice by quiet neutrality." Samuel Johnson

"A celebrity is any well-known TV or movie star who looks like he spends more than two hours working on his hair." Steve Martin

Chapter 31 Chance

"I will prepare and someday my chance will come." Abraham Lincoln

"Read the best books first, or you may not have a chance to read them at all." Henry David Thoreau

"There is no chance and anarchy in the universe. All is system and gradation. Every god is there sitting in his sphere." Ralph Waldo Emerson

"Refusing to ask for help when you need it is refusing someone the chance to be helpful." Ric Ocasek

"A wise man turns chance into good fortune." Thomas FullerMan

"Luck is not chance, it's toil; fortune's expensive smile is earned." Emily Dickinson

"The longer you play, the better chance the better player has of winning." Jack Nicklaus

"One chance is all you need." Jesse Owens

"Everyone has a chance to learn, improve, and build up their skills." Tom Peters

"He that leaveth nothing to chance will do few things ill, but he will do very few things." George Savile

Chapter 32 Change

"Change your thoughts and you change your world." Norman Vincent Peale

"Progress is a nice word. But change is its motivator and change has its enemies." Robert F. Kennedy

"It's not that some people have willpower and some don't. It's that some people are ready to change and others are not." James Gordon, M.D.

"Any transition serious enough to alter your definition of self will require not just small adjustments in your way of living and thinking but a full-on metamorphosis." Martha Beck

"Education is the most powerful weapon which you can use to change the world." Nelson Mandela

"Change your life today. Don't gamble on the future, act now, without delay." Simone de Beauvoir

"If you realize that all things change, there is nothing you will try to hold on to. If you are not afraid of dying, there is nothing you cannot achieve." Lao Tzu

"Failure is not fatal, but failure to change might be." John Wooden

"It's the most unhappy people who most fear change." Mignon McLaughlin

"When you blame others, you give up your power to change." Robert Anthony

Chapter 33 Character

"A man's character is his fate." Heraclitus

"Character - the willingness to accept responsibility for one's own life - is the source from which self respect springs." Joan Didion

"People seem not to see that their opinion of the world is also a confession of their character." Ralph Waldo Emerson

"Character cannot be developed in ease and quiet. Only through experience of trial and suffering can the soul be strengthened, ambition inspired, and success achieved." Helen Keller

"An attitude of philosophic doubt, of suspended judgment, is repugnant to the natural man. Belief is an independent joy to him." William Minto

"You can tell the character of every man when you see how he receives praise." Seneca

"Dreams are the touchstones of our character." Henry David Thoreau

"Character, in the long run, is the decisive factor in the life of an individual and of nations alike." Theodore Roosevelt

"Character is more important than talent." Edwin Louis Cole

"Character, not circumstances, makes the man." Booker T. Washington

Chapter 34 Charity

"In charity there is no excess." Sir Francis Bacon

"A society that has more justice is a society that needs less charity." Ralph Nader

"Every good act is charity. A man's true wealth hereafter is the good that he does in this world to his fellows."   Moliere

"True charity is the desire to be useful to others without thought of recompense"   Emanuel Swedenborg

"The qualities most needed are charity and tolerance, not some form of fanatical faith such as is offered to us by the various rampant isms" Bertrand Russell

"The charity that is a trifle to us can be precious to others."   Homer

"A rich man without charity is a rogue; and perhaps it would be no difficult matter to prove that he is also a fool." Henry Fielding

"We ourselves feel that what we are doing is just a drop in the ocean. But if that drop was not in the ocean, I think the ocean would be less because of that missing drop. I do not agree with the big way of doing things." Mother Teresa

"Charity. To love human beings in so far as they are nothing. That is to love them as God does."   Simone Weil

"He who waits to do a great deal of good at once, will never do anything." Samuel Johnson

Chapter 35 Charm

"Charm is the quality in others, that makes us more satisfied with ourselves." Henri Frederic Amiel

"Things forbidden have a secret charm." Tacitus

"There's something about the way of playing a repellent character, that if you can play him with a certain amount of charm, you can get away with a lot." Curtis Armstrong

"There's no secret to working with kids. They either charm you and you can work with them, or they don't charm you and you feel you're stuck with them." Jerome Robbins

"All charming people, I fancy, are spoiled. It is the secret of their attraction." Oscar Wilde

"There is no personal charm so great as the charm of a cheerful temperament." Henry Van Dyke

"We are born charming, fresh and spontaneous and must be civilized before we are fit to participate in society. " Judith Martin

"It is absurd to divide people into good and bad. People are either charming or tedious." Oscar Wilde

"All charming people have something to conceal, usually their total dependence on the appreciation of others." Cyril Connolly

"A man of such obvious and exemplary charm must be a liar." Anita Brookner

"No one has it who isn't capable of genuinely liking others, at least at the actual moment of meeting and speaking. Charm is always genuine; it may be superficial but it isn't false." P.D James

Chapter 36 Children

"You can learn many things from children. How much patience you have, for instance." Franklin P. Jones

"Every child comes with the message that God is not yet discouraged of man." Rabindranath Tagore

"There are no seven wonders of the world in the eyes of a child.   There are seven million." Walt Streightiff

"There can be no keener revelation of a society's soul than the way in which it treats its children." Nelson Mandela

"Parentage is a very important profession, but no test of fitness for it is ever imposed in the interest of the children." George Bernard Shaw

"I take a very practical view of raising children. I put a sign in each of their rooms: "Checkout Time is 18 years."" Erma Bombeck

"Children are remarkable for their intelligence and ardor, for their curiosity, their intolerance of shams, the clarity and ruthlessness of their vision." Aldous Huxley

"A house without books is like a room without windows. No man has a right to bring up his children without surrounding them with books, if he has the means to buy them." Horace Mann

"Children are a wonderful gift. They have an extraordinary capacity to see into the heart of things and to expose sham and humbug for what they are." Desmond Tutu

"Children are the only form of immortality that we can be sure of." Peter Ustinov

Chapter 37 Civilization

"While civilization has been improving our houses, it has not equally improved the men who are to inhabit them. It has created palaces, but it was not so easy to create noblemen and kings." Henry David Thoreau

"The end of the human race will be that it will eventually die of civilization." Ralph Waldo Emerson

"For me, politeness is a sine qua non of civilization." Robert A. Heinlein

"A modern civilization is only possible when it is accepted that singular beings exist and express themselves freely." Tahar Ben Jelloun

"Science has done more for the development of western civilization in one hundred years than Christianity did in eighteen hundred years." John Burroughs

"If mankind were to continue in other than the present barbarism, a new path must be found, a new civilization based on some other method than technology" Clifford D. Simak

"Books are the carriers of civilization. Without books, history is silent, literature dumb, science crippled, thought and speculation at a standstill." Barbara Tuchman

"Civilization is the lamb's skin in which barbarism masquerades." Thomas B. Aldrich

"Civilization is a stream with banks. The stream is sometimes filled with blood from people killing, stealing, shouting and doing the things historians usually record, while on the banks, unnoticed, people build homes, make love, raise children, sing songs, write poetry and even whittle statues. The story of civilization is the story of what happened on the banks. Historians are pessimists because they ignore the banks for the river." Willaim J. Durant

"Civilization is just a slow process of learning to be kind." Charles L. Lucas

Chapter 38 Cliches

"The computing field is always in need of new cliches." Alan Perlis

"Any great truth can -- and eventually will -- be expressed as a cliche -- a cliche is a sure and certain way to dilute an idea. For instance, my grandmother used to say, 'The black cat is always the last one off the fence.' I have no idea what she meant, but at one time, it was undoubtedly true." Solomon Short

"Attempting to get at truth means rejecting stereotypes and cliches." Harold Evans

"Political art expresses the cliches you agree with, unlike propaganda, which expresses the cliches you don't." Brad Holland

"Most of my cliches aren't original." Chuck Knox

"If someone thinks that love and peace is a cliche that must have been left behind in the Sixties, that's his problem. Love and peace are eternal." John Lennon

"Economics is a subject profoundly conducive to cliche, resonant with boredom. On few topics is an American audience so practiced in turning off its ears and minds. And none can say that the response is ill advised." John Kenneth Galbraith

"Is "tired old cliche" one?" Rod Schmidt

"It is a cliche that most cliches are true, but then like most cliches, that cliche is untrue." Stephen Fry

"Cliches remind and reassure us that we're not alone, that other have trod this ground long ago." Miguel Syjuco

Chapter 39 Committees

"If you want to kill any idea in the world, get a committee working on it." Charles Kettering

"Committee - a group of men who individually can do nothing but as a group decide that nothing can be done." Fred Allen

"Can anything be more Un-American than the Un-American committee?" Burt Lancaster

"If Columbus had an advisory committee he would probably still be at the dock." Arthur Goldberg

"A camel is a horse designed by committee." Alec Issigonis

"To get something done a committee should consist of no more than three people, two of whom are absent." Robert Copeland

"If computers get too powerful, we can organize them into committees. That'll do them in." Author Unknown

"A committee can make a decision that is dumber than any of its members." David Coblitz

"A committee is a cul-de-sac down which ideas are lured and then quietly strangled." Sir Barnett Cocks

"There is no monument dedicated to the memory of a committee." Lester J. Pourciau"Common sense is the collection of prejudices acquired by age eighteen." Albert Einstein

"Everybody gets so much information all day long that they lose their common sense." Gertrude Stein

Chapter 40 Common Sense

"Nothing astonishes men so much as common sense and plain dealing." Ralph Waldo Emerson

"All truth, in the long run, is only common sense clarified." Thomas H. Huxley

"Common sense and nature will do a lot to make the pilgrimage of life not too difficult." W. Somerset Maugham

"Common sense is calculation applied to life." Henri Frederic Amiel

"Common sense is genius dressed in its working clothes." Ralph Waldo Emerson

"Science is nothing but developed perception, interpreted intent, common sense rounded out and minutely articulated." George Santayana

"Common sense is instinct. Enough of it is genius." George Bernard Shaw

"Common sense in spite of, not as the result of education." Victor Hugo

Chapter 41 Communication

"I think that new communications are wonderful and I am delighted to be a part of the Internet generation." Judy Collins

"The Internet is not just one thing, it's a collection of things - of numerous communications networks that all speak the same digital language." Jim Clark

"The single biggest problem in communication is the illusion that it has taken place." George Bernard Shaw

"Think like a wise man but communicate in the language of the people." William Butler Yeats

"It seemed rather incongruous that in a society of supersophisticated communication, we often suffer from a shortage of listeners. Refusing to ask for help when you need it is refusing someone the chance to be helpful." Erma Bombeck

"Good communication is as stimulating as black coffee, and just as hard to sleep after." Anne Morrow Lindbergh

"Communication is the real work of leadership." Nitin Nohria

"The more elaborate our means of communication, the less we communicate." Joseph Priestley

"Electric communication will never be a substitute for the face of someone who with their soul encourages another person to be brave and true." Charles Dickens

"First learn the meaning of what you say, and then speak." Epictetus

"Storytellers, by the very act of telling, communicate a radical learning that changes lives and the world: telling stories is a universally accessible means through which people make meaning." Chris Cavanaugh

Chapter 42 Communism

"Communism is like one big phone company." Lenny Bruce

"Communism is in conflict with human nature." Ernest Renan

"I do not believe in Communism any more than you do but there is nothing wrong with the Communists in this country; several of the best friends I have got are Communists" Franklin D. Roosevelt

"I have no concern with any economic criticisms of the communist system; I cannot inquire into whether the abolition of private property is expedient or advantageous. But I am able to recognize that the psychological premises on which the system is based are an untenable illusion. In abolishing private property we deprive the human love of aggression of one of its instruments... but we have in no way altered the differences in power and influence which are misused by aggressiveness." Sigmund Freud

"The theory of the Communists may be summed up in the single sentence: Abolition of private property." Karl Marx

"In the end we beat them with Levi 501 jeans. Seventy-two years of Communist indoctrination and propaganda was drowned out by a three-ounce Sony Walkman. A huge totalitarian system has been brought to its knees because nobody wants to wear Bulgarian shoes. Now they're lunch, and we're number one on the planet." P.J O'Rourke

"Communism is like prohibition, it is a good idea, but it won't work." Will Rogers

"Under capitalism, man exploits man. Under communism, it's just the opposite." John Kenneth Galbraith

"Capitalism and communism stand at opposite poles. Their essential difference is this: The communist, seeing the rich man and his fine home, says: 'No man should have so much.' The capitalist, seeing the same thing, says: 'All men should have so much.'" Thomas Sowell

"A communist is like a crocodile: when it opens its mouth you cannot tell whether it is trying to smile or preparing to eat you up." Winston Churchill

Chapter 43 Community

"My view is that good community management is like having good municipal government: You should be able to have dissenting opinions and so on, freedom of speech, but your grandmother should also be able to walk down the street at night without having to worry about getting mugged." Jimmy Wales

"I used to be a classic workaholic, and after seeing how little work and career really mean when you reach the end of your life, I put a new emphasis on things I believe count more. These things include: family, friends, being part of a community, and appreciating the little joys of the average day." Mitch Albom

"No other investment yields as great a return as the investment in education. An educated workforce is the foundation of every community and the future of every economy." Brad Henry

"You can have the best technology in the world, but if you don't have a community who wants to use it and who are excited about it, then it has no purpose." Chris Hughes

"We started off trying to set up a small anarchist community, but people wouldn't obey the rules." Alan Bennett

"A community is a group of people who have come together, and they work and they live to try and improve the standard of living and quality of life - and I don't mean money." William Baldwin

"The impersonal hand of government can never replace the helping hand of a neighbor." Hubert H. Humphrey

"Each of us is a being in himself and a being in society, each of us needs to understand himself and understand others, take care of others and be taken care of himself." Haniel Long

"On this shrunken globe, men can no longer live as strangers." Adlai E. Stevenson

"We cannot live only for ourselves.   A thousand fibers connect us with our fellow men."   Herman Melville

"The single most important thing a city can do is provide a community where interesting, smart people want to live with their families." Malcolm Gladwell

Chapter 44 Competence

"The single most exciting thing you encounter in government is competence, because it's so rare." Daniel Patrick Moynihan

"Competence, like truth, beauty, and contact lenses, is in the eye of the beholder." Laurence J. Peter

"The end of education is to see men made whole, both in competence and in conscience." John Dickey

"Never ascribe to malice that which can adequately be explained by incompetence" Napoleon Bonaparte

"A competent and self-confident person is incapable of jealousy in anything. Jealousy is invariably a symptom of neurotic insecurity." Robert A. Heinlein

"No letters after your name are ever going to be a total guarantee of competence any more than they are a guarantee against fraud. Improving competence involves continuing professional development ... That is the really crucial thing, not just passing an examination." Colette Bowe

"Violence is the last refuge of the incompetent." Isaac Asimov

"A king, realizing his incompetence, can either delegate or abdicate his duties. A father can do neither. If only sons could see the paradox, they would understand the dilemma." Marlene Dietrich

"A competent leader can get efficient service from poor troops, while on the contrary an incapable leader can demoralize the best of troops." John J Pershing

"Avoid competency traps. Do not stay only where you are good at things, Go out and be challenged." Andrew Creighton

Chapter 45 Computers

"People think computers will keep them from making mistakes. They're wrong. With computers you make mistakes faster." Adam Osborne

"The real danger is not that computers will begin to think like men, but that men will begin to think like computers." Sydney J. Harris

"Computers are magnificent tools for the realization of our dreams, but no machine can replace the human spark of spirit, compassion, love, and understanding." Louis Gerstner

"Home computers are being called upon to perform many new functions, including the consumption of homework formerly eaten by the dog." Doug Larson

"To err is human - and to blame it on a computer is even more so." Robert Orben

"Anyone who has lost track of time when using a computer knows the propensity to dream, the urge to make dreams come true and the tendency to miss lunch." Tim Berners

"Putting a computer in front of a child and expecting it to teach him is like putting a book under his pillow, only more expensive." Anonymous

"Part of the inhumanity of the computer is that, once it is competently programmed and working smoothly, it is completely honest." Isaac Asimov

"If the automobile had followed the same development cycle as the computer, a Rolls-Royce would today cost $ 100, get a million miles per gallon, and explode once a year, killing everyone inside." Robert X. Cringely

"A computer once beat me at chess, but it was no match for me at kick boxing." Emo Philips

"The question of whether a computer can think is no more interesting than the question of whether a submarine can swim." Edsger Dijkstra

Chapter 46 Conceit

"Conceit is God's gift to little men" Bruce Barton

"Pride and conceit were the original sins of man." Alain Rene Lesage

"Conceit may puff a man up, but never prop him up." John Ruskin

"Calm self-confidence is as far from conceit as the desire to earn a decent living is remote from greed." Channing Pollock

"Conceit, more rich in matter than in words, Brags of his substance, not of ornament. They are but beggars that can count their worth; but my true love is grown to such excess I cannot sum up sum of half my wealth." William Shakespeare

"I don't at all like knowing what people say of me behind my back. It makes me far too conceited." Oscar Wilde

"I've never any pity for conceited people, because I think they carry their comfort about with them." George Eliot

"Frivolity is inborn, conceit acquired by education." Marcus Tullius Cicero

"There is a difference between conceit and confidence. Conceit is bragging about yourself. Confidence means you believe you can get the job done." Johnny Unitas

"Conceit is an insuperable obstacle to all progress." Ellen Terry

Chapter 47 Concentration

"Concentration comes out of a combination of confidence and hunger." Arnold Palmer

"All you need in this life is ignorance and confidence; then success is sure." Mark Twain

"Self-confidence is the first requisite to great undertakings." Samuel Johnson

"My intent is simply to know my material so well that I'm very comfortable with it. Confidence, not perfection, is the goal." Scott Berkun

"Confidence is 10% hard work and 90% delusion." Tina Fey

"Having once decided to achieve a certain task, achieve it at all costs of tedium and distaste. The gain in self-confidence of having accomplished a tiresome labor is immense." Arnold Bennett

"Health is the greatest possession. Contentment is the greatest treasure. Confidence is the greatest friend. Non-being is the greatest joy." Lao Tzu

"If you have no confidence in self, you are twice defeated in the race of life." Marcus Garvey

"To walk around with an ego is a bad thing. To have confidence in yourself is a great thing." Fred Durst

"Whatever we expect with confidence becomes our own self-fulfilling prophecy." Brian Tracy

Chapter 48 Congress

"Talk is cheap - except when congress does it." Cullen Hightower

"Suppose you were an idiot and suppose you were a member of Congress. But I repeat myself." Mark Twain

"This country has come to feel the same when Congress is in session as when the baby gets hold of a hammer." Will Rogers

"I have been up to see the Congress and they do not seem to be able to do anything except to eat peanuts and chew tobacco, while my army is starving." Robert E. Lee

"The American Republic will endure until the day Congress discovers that it can bribe the public with the public's money"   Alexis de Tocqueville

"I have come to the conclusion that one useless man is called a disgrace, that two are called a law firm, and that three or more become a congress"   Peter Stone

"It is the duty of the President to propose and it is the privilege of the Congress to dispose"   Franklin D. Roosevelt

"Congress is so strange. A man gets up to speak and says nothing. Nobody listens - and then everybody disagrees."   Boris Marshalov

"Congress is continually appointing fact-finding committees, when what we really need are some fact-facing committees." Roger Allen

"We will all be better citizens when voting records of our Congressmen are followed as carefully as scores of pro-football games." Lou Erickson

Chapter 49 Conscience

"Never do anything against conscience, even if the state demands it"
Albert Einstein

"Conscience is the inner voice that warns us somebody may be looking." John Lyly

"Conscience is a man's compass." Vincent van Gogh

"Conscience is a mother-in-law whose visit never ends." H. L. Mencken

"Rules of society are nothing; ones conscience is the umpire." Madame Dudevant

"A peace above all earthly dignities, a still and quiet conscience." William Shakespeare

"A lot of people mistake a short memory for a clear conscience." Doug Larson

"Conscience is the mirror of our souls, which represents the errors of our lives in their full shape." George Bancroft

"There is no self-delusion more fatal than that which makes the conscience dreamy with the anodyne of lofty sentiments, while the life is groveling and sensual." James Russell Lowell

"Every human has four endowments- self-awareness, conscience, independent will and creative imagination. These give us the ultimate human freedom... The power to choose, to respond, to change." Stephen R. Covey

Chapter 50 Conservatives

"Conservatives are not necessarily stupid, but most stupid people are conservatives." John Stuart Mill

"The trouble with radicals is that they only read radical literature, and the trouble with conservatives is that they don't read anything" Thomas Nixon Carver

"A conservative is a man with two perfectly good legs who, however, has never learned to walk forward." Franklin D. Roosevelt

"When you are right you cannot be too radical; when you are wrong, you cannot be too conservative." Martin Luther King Jr.

"A conservative is a man who sits and thinks, mostly sits." Woodrow Wilson

"I never dared to be radical when young for fear it would make me conservative when old." Robert Frost

"I'm a conservative, but I'm not a nut about it." George H. W. Bush

"We, as conservative intellectuals, should not be in the business of making excuses for bad parliamentary decisions by Republican leaders in Congress." David Frum

"I do not know which makes a man more conservative - to know nothing but the present, or nothing but the past." John Maynard Keynes

"A conservative is someone who believes in reform. But not now." Mort Sahl

Chapter 51 Conversation

"I often quote myself. It adds spice to my conversation." George Bernard Shaw

"Let us make a special effort to stop communicating with each other, so we can have some conversation." Judith Martin

"The character of a man is known from his conversations." Menander

"Conversation should be pleasant without scurrility, witty without affectation, free without indecency, learned without conceitedness, novel without falsehood." William Shakespeare

"A single conversation across the table with a wise man is better than ten years mere study of books." Henry Wadsworth Longfellow

"Silence is one of the great arts of conversation." Marcus Tullius Cicero

"Polite conversation is rarely either." Fran Lebowitz

"In conversation, humor is worth more than wit and easiness more than knowledge." George Herber

"Conversation would be vastly improved by the constant use of four simple words: I do not know." Andre Maurois

"The first ingredient in conversation is truth, the next good sense, the third good humor, and the fourth wit." William Temple

Chapter 52 Courage

Keep your fears to yourself, but share your courage with others."
Robert Louis Stevenson

"Courage and perseverance have a magical talisman, before which difficulties disappear and obstacles vanish into air." John Quincy Adams

"Life shrinks or expands in proportion to one's courage." Anais Nin

"Any intelligent fool can make things bigger and more complex... It takes a touch of genius - and a lot of courage to move in the opposite direction." Albert Einstein

"Efforts and courage are not enough without purpose and direction." John F. Kennedy

"Courage is the most important of all the virtues, because without courage you can't practice any other virtue consistently. You can practice any virtue erratically, but nothing consistently without courage." Maya Angelou

"Faced with what is right, to leave it undone shows a lack of courage." Confucius

"Success is never final, failure is never fatal. It's courage that counts." John Wooden

"Courage is a mean with regard to fear and confidence." Aristotle

Chapter 53 Coward

"He who despairs over an event is a coward, but he who holds hope for the human condition is a fool." Albert Camus

"Cowards die many times before their deaths; the valiant never taste of death but once." William Shakespeare

"The real hero is always a hero by mistake; he dreams of being an honest coward like everybody else." Umberto Eco

"Cowardice and courage are never without a measure of affectation. Nor is love. Feelings are never true. They play with their mirrors." Jean Baudrillard

"Fear has its use but cowardice has none." Mahatma Gandhi

"To sin by silence when they should protest makes cowards of men." Abraham Lincoln

"It is better to be the widow of a hero than the wife of a coward." Dolores Ibarruri

"Cowardice ... is almost always simply a lack of ability to suspend the functioning of the imagination." Ernest Hemingway

"The opposite of courage in our society is not cowardice, it is conformity." Rollo May

"A light supper, a good night's sleep, and a fine morning have often made a hero of the same man who, by indigestion, a restless night, and a rainy morning would have proved a coward" Lord Chesterfield

Chapter 54 Creativity

"Creativity requires the courage to let go of certainties." Erich Fromm

"Success is that old ABC - ability, breaks, and courage" Charles Luckman

"Creativity can solve almost any problem. The creative act, the defeat of habit by originality, overcomes everything." George Lois

"To live a creative life, we must lose our fear of being wrong." Joseph Chilton Pearce

"Creativity represents a miraculous coming together of the uninhibited energy of the child with its apparent opposite and enemy, the sense of order imposed on the disciplined adult intelligence." Norman Podhoretz

"The creative person is both more primitive and more cultivated, more destructive, a lot madder and a lot saner, than the average person." Frank Barron

"Creativity is the ability to see relationships where none exist." Thomas Disch

"Creativity is a lot like looking at the world through a kaleidoscope. You look at a set of elements, the same ones everyone else sees, but then reassemble those floating bits and pieces into an enticing new possibility. Effective leaders are able to" Rosabeth Moss Kanter

"Creativity is inventing, experimenting, growing, taking risks, breaking rules, making mistakes, and having fun." Mary Lou Cook

"Energy is the key to creativity. Energy is the key to life." William Shatner

"Creativity is a natural extension of our enthusiasm." Earl Nightingale

"Success is fickle, but creativity is a gift." Tommy Shaw

Chapter 55 Crime

"Organized crime in America takes in over forty billion dollars a year and spends very little on office supplies." Woody Allen

"When you think of the long and gloomy history of man, you will find more hideous crimes have been committed in the name of obedience than have ever been committed in the name of rebellion." C. P. Snow

"A crime which is the crime of many none avenge." Lucan

"He who does not prevent a crime when he can, encourages it." Seneca

"And who are the greater criminals--those who sell the instruments of death, or those who buy them and use them?" Robert Emmet Sherwood

"We don't seem to be able to check crime, so why not legalize it and then tax it out of business." Will Rogers

"All crime is a kind of disease and should be treated as such." Mahatma Gandhi

"I constantly remind people that crime isn't solved by technology; it's solved by people." Patricia Cornwell

"If it is committed in the name of God or country, there is no crime so heinous that the public will not forgive it." Tom Robbins

"It's about time law enforcement got as organized as organized crime." Rudy Giuliani

Chapter 56 Curiosity

"It is a miracle that curiosity survives formal education." Albert Einstein

"Curiosity is the very basis of education and if you tell me that curiosity killed the cat, I say only the cat died nobly." Arnold Edinborough

"The important thing is not to stop questioning. Curiosity has its own reason for existing. One cannot help but be in awe when he contemplates the mysteries of eternity, of life, of the marvelous structure of reality. It is enough if one tries merely to comprehend a little of this mystery every day. Never lose a holy curiosity." Albert Einstein

"Curiosity is one of the permanent and certain characteristics of a vigorous mind." Samuel Johnson

"Curiosity is the wick in the candle of learning." William Arthur Ward

"When you're curious, you find lots of interesting things to do." Walt Disney

"Curiosity is lying in wait for every secret." Ralph Waldo Emerson

"A good scientist is a person in whom the childhood quality of perennial curiosity lingers on. Once he gets an answer, he has other questions." Frederick Seitz

"Curiosity will conquer fear even more than bravery will." James Stephens

"Seize the moment of excited curiosity on any subject to solve your doubts; for if you let it pass, the desire may never return, and you may remain in ignorance." William Wirt

Chapter 57 Cynicism

"Idealism is what precedes experience; cynicism is what follows."
David T. Wolf

"A cynic is a man who, when he smells flowers, looks around for a coffin." H. L. Mencken

"A cynic is not merely one who reads bitter lessons from the past, he is one who is prematurely disappointed in the future." Sidney J. Harris

"It's hard to argue against cynics - they always sound smarter than optimists because they have so much evidence on their side" Molly Ivins

 "Modern cynics and skeptics... see no harm in paying those to whom they entrust the minds of their children a smaller wage than is paid to those to whom they entrust the care of their plumbing." John Fitzgerald Kennedy

"Do not crush the flowers of wisdom with the hobnail boots of cynicism." Bill Bailey

"The cynic is one who never sees a good quality in a man, and never fails to see a bad one. He is the human owl, vigilant in darkness and blind to light, mousing for vermin, and never seeing noble game." Henry Ward Beecher

"Cynicism is the intellectual cripple's substitute for intelligence." Russell Lynes

"The only deadly sin I know is cynicism." Henry Lewis Stimson

"I worry that no matter how cynical you become, it's never enough to keep up." Jane Wagner

Chapter 58 Dance

"When I dance, the sun sails safely through the night; when I dance, the future is formed by my feet; when I dance, and the stars move through the heavens; when I dance, Venus shimmers the desert; when I dance, dust becomes silver, and stones are made of gold!" Cosi Fabian

"If I could tell you what it meant, there would be no point in dancing it." Isadora Duncan

"Dance is the hidden language of the soul of the body." Martha Graham

"Dancing: The vertical expression of a horizontal desire legalized by music." George Bernard Shaw

"To dance is to be in tune with the steps of life." Sasha Azevedo

"I do not try to dance better than anyone else. I only try to dance better than myself." Mikhail Baryshnikov

"On with the dance! Let joy be unconfined" Lord Byron

"Dancing is the poetry of the foot." John Dryden

"I would not know what the spirit of a philosopher might wish more to be than a good dancer." Friedrich Nietzsche

"Every day brings a chance for you to draw in a breath, kick off your shoes, and dance." Oprah Winfrey

Chapter 59 Death

"Death is nothing to us, since when we are, death has not come, and when death has come, we are not." Epicurus

"Do not fear death so much, but rather the inadequate life." Bertolt Brecht

"The fear of death follows from the fear of life. A man who lives fully is prepared to die at any time." Mark Twain

"Life is hard. Then you die. Then they throw dirt in your face. Then the worms eat you. Be grateful it happens in that order." David Gerrold

"Our dead are never dead to us, until we have forgotten them." George Eliot

"From my rotting body, flowers shall grow and I am in them and that is eternity." Edvard Munch

"Because of indifference, one dies before one actually dies." Elie Wiesel

"He who doesn't fear death dies only once." Giovanni Falcone

"I am not afraid of death, I just don't want to be there when it happens." Woody Allen

"No one wants to die. Even people who want to go to heaven don't want to die to get there. And yet death is the destination we all share. No one has ever escaped it. And that is as it should be, because Death is very likely the single best invention of Life. It is Life's change agent. It clears out the old to make way for the new." Steve Job

Chapter 60 Decisions

"We are given one life, and the decision is ours whether to wait for circumstances to make up our mind or whether to act and, in acting, to live." Omar Nelson Bradley

"Most of our executives make very sound decisions. The trouble is many of them have turned out not to have been right." Bullock, Donald

"Shelving hard decisions is the least ethical course." Adrian Cadbury

"Indecision and delays are the parents of failure." George A. Canning

"The more alternatives, the more difficult the choice." Abbe' D'Allanival

"If you limit your choices only to what seems possible or reasonable, you disconnect yourself from what you truly want, and all that is left is a compromise." Robert Fritz

"In any moment of decision, the best thing you can do is the right thing, the next best thing is the wrong thing, and the worst thing you can do is nothing." Theodore Roosevelt

"The risk of a wrong decision is preferable to the terror of indecision." Maimonides

"On the plains of hesitation bleach the bones of countless millions who, at the dawn of decision, sat down to wait, and waiting died." Sam Ewing

"The politician who never made a mistake never made a decision." John Major

Chapter 61 Defeat

"Victory has a thousand fathers, but defeat is an orphan." John F. Kennedy

"The greatest test of courage on earth is to bear defeat without losing heart." Robert Green Ingersoll

"I contend that not only can you laugh at adversity, but it is essential to do so if you are to deal with setbacks without defeat." Allen Klein

"Defeat should never be a source of discouragement but rather a fresh stimulus." Robert South

"You can learn a line from a win and a book from a defeat." Paul Brown

"You may glory in a team triumphant... But you fall in love with a team in defeat." Roger Kahn

"To expect defeat is nine-tenths of defeat itself." Francis Marion Crawford

"There are some defeats more triumphant than victories." Michel de Montaigne

"Victory attained by violence is tantamount to a defeat, for it is momentary." Mahatma Gandhi

"What is defeat? Nothing but education; nothing but the first step to something better." Wendell Phillips

Chapter 62 Design

"In most people's vocabularies, design means veneer. It's interior decorating. It's the fabric of the curtains of the sofa. But to me, nothing could be further from the meaning of design. Design is the fundamental soul of a human-made creation that ends up expressing itself in successive outer layers of the product or service." Steve Jobs

"Design works if it's authentic, inspired, and has a clear point of view. It can't be a collection of input." Ron Johnson

"Design can never be an ultimate explanation for anything. It can only be a proximate explanation. A plane or a car is explained by a designer but that's because the designer himself, the engineer, is explained by natural selection." Richard Dawkins

"Book-jacket design may become a lost art, like album-cover design, without which late-20th-century iconography would have been pauperized." James Wolcott

"A purpose, an intention, a design, strikes everywhere even the careless, the most stupid thinker." David Hume

"Design is so critical it should be on the agenda of every meeting in every single department." Tom Peters

"A person should design the way he makes a living around how he wishes to make a life." Charlie Byrd

"It is relatively easy to design for the perfect cases, when everything goes right, or when all the information required is available in proper format." Donald Norman

"The details are not the details. They make the design." Charles Eames

"Technology is making design more exciting, with color, wallpaper, textures, fabrics that could never have been created without the technology." David Bromstad

Chapter 63 Desire

"He who desires is always poor." Claudianus

"Let your desires be ruled by reason." Cicero

"In order to succeed, your desire for success should be greater than your fear of failure." Bill Cosby

"It is for us to pray not for tasks equal to our powers, but for powers equal to our tasks, to go forward with a great desire forever beating at the door of our hearts as we travel toward our distant goal." Helen Keller

"If you're bored with life - you don't get up every morning with a burning desire to do things - you don't have enough goals." Lou Holtz

"Life contains but two tragedies. One is not to get your heart's desire; the other is to get it." George Bernard Shaw

"All progress is based upon a universal innate desire on the part of every organism to live beyond its income." Samuel Butler

"Desire is the starting point of all achievement, not a hope, not a wish, but a keen pulsating desire which transcends everything." Napoleon Hill

"The desire to know is natural to good men." Leonardo da Vinci

"Desire is half of life; indifference is half of death." Kahlil Gibran

Chapter 64 Destiny

**"A person often meets his destiny on the road he took to avoid it."
Jean de La Fontaine**

"Destiny is no matter of chance. It is a matter of choice: It is not a thing to be waited for, it is a thing to be achieved." William Jennings Bryan

"Sow a thought, and you reap an act; Sow an act, and you reap a habit; Sow a habit, and you reap a character; Sow a character, and you reap a destiny" Charles Reade

"Every man has his own destiny: the only imperative is to follow it, to accept it, no matter where it leads him." Henry Miller

"We are made for larger ends than Earth can encompass. Oh, let us be true to our exalted destiny." Catherine Booth

"And the high destiny of the individual is to serve rather than to rule, or to impose himself in any other way." Albert Einstein

"The destiny of man is in his own soul." Herodotus

"Our problems are man-made, therefore they may be solved by man. No problem of human destiny is beyond human beings." John F. Kennedy

"A consistent soul believes in destiny, a capricious one in chance." Benjamin Disraeli

"It is a mistake to try to look too far ahead. The chain of destiny can only be grasped one link at a time." Sir Winston Churchill

Chapter 65 Differences

"A great marriage is not when the 'perfect couple' comes together. It is when an imperfect couple learns to enjoy their differences." Dave Meurer

"Toward no crime have men shown themselves so cold-bloodedly cruel as in punishing differences of belief." James Russell Lowell

"Honest differences are often a healthy sign of progress." Mahatma Gandhi

"We must not, in trying to think about how we can make a big difference, ignore the small daily differences we can make which, over time, add up to big differences that we often cannot foresee." Marian Wright Edelman

"We are enriched by our reciprocate differences." Paul Valery

"Science, for hundreds of years, has spanned the differences between cultures and between countries." Laurel Clark

"Differences challenge assumptions." Anne Wilson Schaef

"Warfare is an utterly stupid method of settling differences of interest between different nations." George H. Mead

"I find it very beautiful to work in different countries because I see the mentality differences there. It is so rich, one always carries forward something." Michelle Hunziker

"Share our similarities, celebrate our differences." M. Scott Peck

Chapter 66 Dignity

"Let not a man guard his dignity, but let his dignity guard him." Ralph Waldo Emerson

"One's dignity may be assaulted, vandalized and cruelly mocked, but cannot be taken away unless it is surrendered." Michael J. Fox

"No race can prosper till it learns that there is as much dignity in tilling a field as in writing a poem." Booker T. Washington

"Remember this-that there is a proper dignity and proportion to be observed in the performance of every act of life." Marcus Aurelius Antoninus

"It is not wealth one asks for, but just enough to preserve one's dignity, to work unhampered, to be generous, frank and independent." W. Somerset Maugham

"Every man has his dignity. I'm willing to forget mine, but at my own discretion and not when someone else tells me to." Denis Diderot

"If a man happens to find himself, he has a mansion which he can inhabit with dignity all the days of his life." James A. Michener

"When an individual is protesting society's refusal to acknowledge his dignity as a human being, his very act of protest confers dignity on him." Bayard Rustin

"Humor is an affirmation of dignity, a declaration of man's superiority to all that befalls him." Romain Gary

"From the depth of need and despair, people can work together, can organize themselves to solve their own problems and fill their own needs with dignity and strength." Cesar Chavez

Chapter 67 Discovery

"All truths are easy to understand once they are discovered; the point is to discover them." Galileo Galilei

"Man cannot discover new oceans unless he has the courage to lose sight of the shore." Andre Gide

"There is no such thing as the pursuit of happiness, but there is the discovery of joy" Joyce Grenfell

"Discovery consists in seeing what everyone else has seen and thinking what no one else has thought." Albert Szent-Gyorgy

"The progress of science is the discovery at each step of a new order which gives unity to what had seemed unlike" Jacob Bronkowski

"By mutual confidence and mutual aid - great deeds are done, and great discoveries made" Homer

"Mistakes are the portals of discovery." James Joyce

"We discover in others what others hide from us, and we recognize in others what we hide from ourselves." Marquis de Vauvenargues

"Education is a progressive discovery of our own ignorance." Will Durant

"I've made an odd discovery. Every time I talk to a savant I feel quite sure that happiness is no longer a possibility. Yet when I talk with my gardener, I'm convinced of the opposite." Bertrand Russell

Chapter 68 Dogs

"Dogs laugh, but they laugh with their tails." Max Eastman

"A dog is not "almost human" and I know of no greater insult to the canine race than to describe it as such." John Holmes

"The dog is a gentleman; I hope to go to his heaven, not man's." Mark Twain

"A dog is one of the remaining reasons why some people can be persuaded to go for a walk." O.A. Battista

"No philosophers so thoroughly comprehend us as dogs and horses." Herman Melville

"If you are a dog and your owner suggests that you wear a sweater... suggest that he wear a tail." Fran Lebowitz

"Dogs feel very strongly that they should always go with you in the car, in case the need should arise for them to bark violently at nothing right in your ear." Dave Barry

"To sit with a dog on a hillside on a glorious afternoon is to be back in Eden, where doing nothing was not boring - it was peace." Milan Kundera

"The more one gets to know of men, the more one values dogs." Alphonse Toussenel

"If you pick up a starving dog and make him prosperous, he will not bite you. This is the principal difference between a dog and a man." Mark Twain

Chapter 69 Doubt

"It is better to remain silent and be thought a fool than to open one's mouth and remove all doubt." Mark Twain

"Faith and doubt both are needed - not as antagonists, but working side by side to take us around the unknown curve." Lillian Smith

"Modest doubt is called the beacon of the wise." William Shakespeare

"If you would be a real seeker after truth, it is necessary that at least once in your life you doubt, as far as possible, all things." Rene Descartes

"Men become civilized, not in proportion to their willingness to believe, but in proportion to their readiness to doubt." Ambrose Bierce

"Doubt is the vestibule through which all must pass before they can enter into the temple of wisdom." Charles Caleb Colton

"Fanaticism is overcompensation for doubt." Robertson Davies

"Doubt, it seems to me, is the central condition of a human being in the twentieth century." Salman Rushdie

"The intellectual, the man of thought, doubt and analysis, should give the best of himself." Tahar Ben Jelloun

"It is easier to believe than to doubt." Gene Fowler

Chapter 70 Dreams

"You see things; and you say, 'Why?' But I dream things that never were; and I say, 'Why not?'" George Bernard Shaw

"Dreams are illustrations... from the book your soul is writing about you." Marsha Norman

"There are some people who live in a dream world, and there are some who face reality; and then there are those who turn one into the other." Douglas H. Everett

"Each of us has an inner dream that we can unfold if we will just have the courage to admit what it is. And the faith to trust our own admission. The admitting is often very difficult." Julia Cameron

"Do not lose hold of your dreams or aspirations. For if you do, you may still exist but you have ceased to live." Henry David Thoreau

"Dreaming permits each and every one of us to be quietly and safely insane every night of our lives." William Dement

"In a dream you are never eighty." Anne Sexton

"The best reason for having dreams is that in dreams no reasons are necessary." Ashleigh Brilliant

"Nothing much happens without a dream. For something really great to happen, it takes a really great dream." Robert Greenleaf

"A goal is a dream taken seriously." Henry David Thoreau

Chapter 71 Drinking

"I know a man who gave up smoking, drinking, sex, and rich food. He was healthy right up to the day he killed himself." Johnny Carson

"I tried to give up drugs by drinking." Lou Reed

"It's not the drinking to be blamed, but the excess." John Selden

"I began drinking alcohol at the age of thirteen and gave it up in my fifty sixth year; it was like going straight from puberty to a mid-life crisis." George Montgomery

"When I read about the evils of drinking, I gave up reading." Henny Youngman

"One reason I don't drink is that I want to know when I am having a good time." Nancy Astor

"It's always difficult to make conversation with a drunk, and there's no denying it, the sober are at a disadvantage with him." W. Somerset Maugham

"It is better to hide ignorance, but it is hard to do this when we relax over wine." Heraclitus

"Electricity is actually made up of extremely tiny particles called electrons that you cannot see with the naked eye unless you have been drinking." Dave Barry

Chapter 72 Drugs

"Half of the modern drugs could well be thrown out of the window, except that the birds might eat them." Dr. Martin Henry Fischer

"The last time somebody said, 'I find I can write much better with a word processor.' I replied, 'They used to say the same thing about drugs.'" Roy Blount Jr.

"All drugs of any interest to any moderately intelligent person in America are now illegal." Thomas Szasz

"Don't do drugs because if you do drugs you'll go to prison, and drugs are really expensive in prison." John Hardwick

"Drugs are reality's legal loopholes." Jeremy P. Johnson

"Pharma industry is the art of making billions from milligrams." Gerhard Kocher

"Drugs are a waste of time. They destroy your memory and your self-respect and everything that goes along with your self-esteem." Kurt Cobain

"Our national drug is alcohol. We tend to regard the use any other drug with special horror." William S. Burroughs

"I never took hallucinogenic drugs because I never wanted my consciousness expanded one unnecessary iota." Fran Lebowitz

"I don't need drugs to make my life tragic" Eddie Vedder

Chapter 73 Duty

"I know of only one duty, and that is to love." Albert Camus

"Let's have faith that right makes might; and in that faith let us, to the end, dare to do our duty as we understand it." Abraham Lincoln

"Non-cooperation with evil is as much a duty as is cooperation with good." Mahatma Gandhi

"For a man who has done his natural duty, death is as natural as sleep." George Santayana

"Good luck is the willing handmaid of an upright and energetic character, and conscientious observance of duty." James Russell Lowell

"We never fail when we try to do our duty, we always fail when we neglect to do it." Robert Baden-Powell

"No duty is more urgent than that of returning thanks." James Allen

"I think the first duty of society is justice." Alexander Hamilton

"The duty of helping one's self in the highest sense involves the helping of one's neighbors." Samuel Smiles

"Reading should not be presented to children as a chore, a duty. It should be offered as a gift." Kate DiCamillo

Chapter 74 Economics

"An economist is a man who states the obvious in terms of the incomprehensible." Alfred A. Knopf

"Economics is extremely useful as a form of employment for economists." John Kenneth Galbraith

"If all economists were laid end to end, they would not reach a conclusion." George Bernard Shaw

"An economist is a surgeon with an excellent scalpel and a rough-edged lancet, who operates beautifully on the dead and tortures the living." Nicholas Chamfort

"There are 10^{11} stars in the galaxy. That used to be a huge number. But it's only a hundred billion. It's less than the national deficit! We used to call them astronomical numbers. Now we should call them economical numbers." Richard Feynman

"An economist is an expert who will know tomorrow why the things he predicted yesterday didn't happen today." Laurence J. Peter

"I studied economics and made it my career for two reasons. The subject was and is intellectually fascinating and challenging, particularly to someone with taste and talent for theoretical reasoning and quantitative analysis." James Tobin

"Economists are pessimists: they've predicted 8 of the last 3 depressions" Barry Asmus

"The notion that big business and big labor and big government can sit down around a table somewhere and work out the direction of the American economy is at complete variance with the reality of where the American economy is headed. I mean, it's like dinosaurs gathering to talk about the evolution of a new generation of mammals." Bruce Babbit

"Ask five economists and you'll get five different explanations six if one went to Harvard." Edgar R. Fiedler

Chapter 75 Education

"Education is what remains after one has forgotten what one has learned in school." Albert Einstein

"Nations have recently been led to borrow billions for war; no nation has ever borrowed largely for education. Probably, no nation is rich enough to pay for both war and civilization. We must make our choice; we cannot have both." Abraham Flexner

"Education aims to give you a boost up the ladder of knowledge. Too often, it just gives you a cramp on one of its rungs." Martin H. Fischer

"Education is the ability to listen to almost anything without losing your temper or your self-confidence." Robert Frost

"When a subject becomes totally obsolete we make it a required course." Peter Drucker

"I think everyone should go to college and get a degree and then spend six months as a bartender and six months as a cabdriver. Then they would really be educated." Al McGuire

"The tragedy of education is played in two scenes - incompetent pupils facing competent teachers and incompetent teachers facing competent pupils." Martin H. Fischer

"Education: the inculcation of the incomprehensible into the indifferent by the incompetent." John Maynard Keynes

"The one real object of education is to have a man in the condition of continually asking questions." Bishop Mandell Creighton

"A fool's brain digests philosophy into folly, science into superstition, and art into pedantry. Hence University education." George Bernard Shaw

Chapter 76 Emotions

"If you don't manage your emotions, then your emotions will manage you." Doc Childre and Deborah Rozman

"The finest emotion of which we are capable is the mystic emotion." Albert Einstein

"Shame is such an intense emotion. It just can drive you." Kyra Sedgwick

"You cannot demonstrate an emotion or prove an aspiration." John Morley

"When I repress my emotion my stomach keeps score." Enoch Powell

"Music is the shorthand of emotion." Leo Nikolaevich

"It is not because the truth is too difficult to see that we make mistakes... we make mistakes because the easiest and most comfortable course for us is to seek insight where it accords with our emotions - especially selfish ones." Alexander Solzhenitsyn

"The artist is a receptacle for the emotions that come from all over the place: from the sky, from the earth, from a scrap of paper, from a passing shape, from a spider's web." Pablo Picasso

"Just as your car runs more smoothly and requires less energy to go faster and farther when the wheels are in perfect alignment, you perform better when your thoughts, feelings, emotions, goals, and values are in balance." Brian Tracy

"People don't ask for facts in making up their minds. They would rather have one good, soul-satisfying emotion than a dozen facts." Robert Keith Leavitt

Chapter 77 Enemies

"Always forgive your enemies - nothing annoys them so much." Oscar Wilde

"A friend is one who has the same enemies as you have" Abraham Lincoln

"Now, now my good man, this is no time for making enemies." [Voltaire on his deathbed in response to a priest asking that he renounce Satan] Voltaire

"You can discover what your enemy fears most by observing the means he uses to frighten you." Eric Hoffer

"He who has a thousand friends has not a friend to spare, and he who has one enemy will meet him everywhere." Ralph Waldo Emerson

"Forgive your enemies, but never forget their names" John Fitzgerald Kennedy

"Instead of loving your enemies - treat your friends a little better." Edward W. Howe

"When we turn to one another for counsel we reduce the number of our enemies." Khalil Gibran

"If you want peace, you don't talk to your friends. You talk to your enemies." Desmond Tutu

Chapter 78 Energy

"Energy and persistence conquer all things." Benjamin Franklin

"The energy of the mind is the essence of life." Aristotle

"Goals provide the energy source that powers our lives. One of the best ways we can get the most from the energy we have is to focus it. That is what goals can do for us; concentrate our energy." Denis Waitley

"The more you lose yourself in something bigger than yourself, the more energy you will have." Norman Vincent Peale

"Real wealth is ideas plus energy." Richard Buckminster Fuller

"I have learned through bitter experience the one supreme lesson to conserve my anger, and as heat conserved is transmitted into energy, even so our anger controlled can be transmitted into a power that can move the world." Mahatma Gandhi

"Feeling sorry for yourself, and you present condition, is not only a waste of energy but the worst habit you could possibly have." Dale Carnegie

"Most people spend more time and energy going around problems than in trying to solve them." Henry Ford

"All the breaks you need in life wait within your imagination, Imagination is the workshop of your mind, capable of turning mind energy into accomplishment and wealth." Napoleon Hill

"Nobody realizes that some people expend tremendous energy merely to be normal." Albert Camus

"It takes as much energy to wish as it does to plan." Eleanor Roosevelt

"Determination, energy, and courage appear spontaneously when we care deeply about something. We take risks that are unimaginable in any other context." Margaret J. Wheatley

Chapter 79 Engineering

"Engineering is the art of organizing and directing men and controlling the forces and materials of nature for the benefit of the human race." Henry G. Stott

"Engineers participate in the activities which make the resources of nature available in a form beneficial to man and provide systems which will perform optimally and economically." L. M. K. Boelter

"The ideal engineer is a composite ... He is not a scientist, he is not a mathematician, he is not a sociologist or a writer; but he may use the knowledge and techniques of any or all of these disciplines in solving engineering problems." N. W. Dougherty

"The engineering is secondary to the vision." Cynthia Ozick

"Leonardo Da Vinci combined art and science and aesthetics and engineering, that kind of unity is needed once again." Ben Shneiderman

"With engineering, I view this year's failure as next year's opportunity to try it again. Failures are not something to be avoided. You want to have them happen as quickly as you can so you can make progress rapidly." Gordon Moore

"I'm quite into the idea of engineering being beautiful." Sean Booth

"The human foot is a masterpiece of engineering and a work of art." Leonardo da Vinci

"One man's "magic" is another man's engineering. "Supernatural" is a null word." Robert A. Heinlein

"A good engineer thinks in reverse and asks himself about the stylistic consequences of the components and systems he proposes." Helmut Jahn

Chapter 80 England

"England and America are two countries separated by a common language." George Bernard Shaw

"If you want to eat well in England, eat three breakfasts." W. Somerset Maugham

"In England, we have such good manners that if someone says something impolite, the police will get involved." Russell Brand

"Coffee in England is just toasted milk." Christopher Fry

"In England only uneducated people show off their knowledge; nobody quotes Latin or Greek authors in the course of conversation, unless he has never read them." George Mikes

"England is my wife, America my mistress. It is very good sometimes to get away from one's wife." Cedric Hardwicke

"The whole strength of England lies in the fact that the enormous majority of the English people are snobs" George Bernard Shaw

"The people of England are the most enthusiastic in the world." Benjamin Disraeli

"In England we have come to rely upon a comfortable time-lag of fifty years or a century intervening between the perception that something ought to be done and a serious attempt to do it." H. G. Wells

"In England there are sixty different religions, and only one sauce" Francesco Caraccio

Chapter 81 Environment

"It's time we stopped ignoring the environment. Let's not let another election go by without making this a high priority." David Suzuki

"The whole purpose was to say that it doesn't have to be a zero sum. It's not the environment or jobs. You can have both. You can help the auto industry achieve that if you have investment in plants." Jennifer Granholm

"We owe it to ourselves and to the next generation to conserve the environment so that we can bequeath our children a sustainable world that benefits all." Wangari Maathai

"I can find God in nature, in animals, in birds and the environment." Pat Buckley

"Chimpanzees, gorillas, orangutans have been living for hundreds of thousands of years in their forest, living fantastic lives, never overpopulating, never destroying the forest. I would say that they have been in a way more successful than us as far as being in harmony with the environment." Jane Goodall

"We don't have to sacrifice a strong economy for a healthy environment." Dennis Weaver

"We are on the precipice of climate system tipping points beyond which there is no redemption." James Hansen

"We do not inherit the earth from our ancestors, we borrow it from our children." Native American saying

"Some scientists are predicting by 2050, only 8% of biomes [plants and animals] will be left in their original habitats." Dr. Sally Aiken

"We stand now where two roads diverge. But unlike the roads in Robert Frost's familiar poem, they are not equally fair. The road we have long been traveling is deceptively easy, a smooth superhighway on which we progress with great speed, but at its end lies disaster. The other fork of the road — the one less traveled by — offers our last, our only chance to reach a destination that assures the preservation of the earth." Rachel Carson

Chapter 82 Equality

"Before God we are all equally wise - and equally foolish." Albert Einstein

"As men, we are all equal in the presence of death." Publilius Syrus

"Equality is the soul of liberty; there is, in fact, no liberty without it." Frances Wright

"Equality is the public recognition, effectively expressed in institutions and manners, of the principle that an equal degree of attention is due to the needs of all human beings." Simone Weil

"I happen to agree with many of the liberal emphasis on compassion, justice and equality. I just disagree that it's the government's role to provide everything." Rick Warren

"The liberal ideal is that everyone should have fair access and fair opportunity. This is not equality of result. It's equality of opportunity. There's a fundamental difference." Robert Reich

"As experience widens, one begins to see how much on a level human things are." Joseph Farrell

"The longer we live, the more we find out we are like other persons." Oliver Wendell Holmes

"Men are born equal, but they are also born different." Erich Fromm

"It is the mark of the cultured man that he is aware of the fact that equality is an ethical and not a biological principle." Ashley Montagu

"Between persons of equal income there is no distinction except distinctions of merit. Money is nothing: character, conduct and capacity are everything. There would be great people and ordinary people and little people, but the great would always be those who had done great things, and never the idiots whose mothers had spoiled them and whose fathers had left them a hundred thousand a year; and the little would be persons of small minds and mean characters, and not the poor persons who had never had a chance. That is why idiots are always in favor of inequality of income (their only chance of eminence), and the really great in favor of equality." George Bernard Shaw

Chapter 83 Etiquette

"Etiquette means behaving yourself a little better than in absolutely essential." Will Cuppy"

"Etiquette requires us to admire the human race." Mark Twain.

"Etiquette is the ceremonial code of polite life, more voluminous and minute in each portion of society according to its rank." John Ramsay McCulloch

"Those who have mastered etiquette, who are entirely, impeccably right, would seem to arrive at a point of exquisite dullness." Dorothy Parker

"Etiquette has no regard for moral qualities" Douglas William Jerrold

"Nothing more rapidly inclines a person to go into a monastery than reading a book on etiquette. There are so many trivial ways in which it is possible to commit some social sin." Quentin Crisp

"Etiquette is the invention of wise men to keep fools at a distance." Sir Richard Steele

"The world was my oyster but I used the wrong fork." Oscar Wilde

"Life be not so short but that there is always time for courtesy." Ralph Waldo Emerson

"Don't reserve your best behavior for special occasions. You can't have two sets of manners, two social codes – one for those you admire and want to impress, another for those whom you consider unimportant. You must be the same to all people." Lillian Eichler Watson

Chapter 84 Evil

"Men never do evil so completely and cheerfully as when they do it from religious conviction." Blaise Pascal

"Every minute you are thinking of evil, you might have been thinking of good instead. Refuse to pander to a morbid interest in your own misdeeds. Pick yourself up, be sorry, shake yourself, and go on again." Evelyn Underhill

"Evil when we are in its power is not felt as evil but as a necessity, or even a duty." Simone Weil

"A person may cause evil to others not only by his action but by his inaction, and in either case he is justly accountable to them for the injury." John Stuart Mill

"No man is justified in doing evil on the ground of expediency." Theodore Roosevelt

Chapter 85 Excellence

"Be a yardstick of quality. Some people aren't used to an environment where excellence is expected." Steve Jobs

"Excellence is an art won by training and habituation. We do not act rightly because we have virtue or excellence, but we rather have those because we have acted rightly. We are what we repeatedly do. Excellence, then, is not an act but a habit." Aristotle

"Excellence is to do a common thing in an uncommon way." Booker T. Washington

"Whoever I am, or whatever I am doing, some kind of excellence is within my reach." John W. Gardner

"Next to excellence is the appreciation of it." William Makepeace Thackeray

"My philosophy all my life has been the pursuit of excellence." John Kluge

"If you want people to listen, you have to have a platform to speak from, and that is excellence in what you do." William Pollard

"Excellence is a process that should occupy all our days." Ted W. Engstrom

"Life's like a play; it's not the length but the excellence of the acting that matters." Seneca

"If you are going to achieve excellence in big things, you develop the habit in little matters. Excellence is not an exception, it is a prevailing attitude." Colin Powell

Chapter 86 Exercise

"Worrying about your gray hair when your weight's soaring out of control is like mowing your lawn while your house is on fire." Edward Ugel

"Exercise along provides psychological and physical benefits. Hoever, if you also adopt a strategy that engages your mind while you exercise, you can get a whole host of psychological benefits fairly quickly." James Rippe

"Walking is the best possible exercise. Habituate yourself to walk very far." Thomas Jefferson

"If you're asking your kids to exercise, then you better do it, too. Practice what you preach." Bruce Jenner

"Find fitness with fun dancing. It is fun and makes you forget about the dreaded exercise." Paula Abdul

"A lot of exercise is mindless; you can have music or the radio on and not be aware. But if you're aware in anything you do – and it doesn't have to be yoga – it changes you. Being present changes you." Mariel Hemingway

"You can't exercise your way out of a bad diet." Mark Hyman

"Exercise should be regarded as tribute to the heart." Gene Tunney

"Exercise is the chief source of improvement in our faculties." Hugh Blair

"It seems every year, people make the resolution to exercise and lose weight and get in shape." Ed Smith

"You need to eat normally and healthfully, and you need to exercise. I'm so passionate about this because I think people spend their lives not happy in their bodies." Courtney Thorne Smith

Chapter 87 Experience

"We know nothing of what will happen in the future, but in the analogy of experience." Abraham Lincoln

"Experience teaches only the teachable." Aldous Huxley

"Experience is a hard teacher because she gives the test first, the lesson afterwards." Vernon Sanders Law

"Nothing is a waste of time if you use the experience wisely." Auguste Rodin

"Experience is the teacher of all things." Julius Caesar

"Good judgment comes from experience, and experience comes from bad judgment." Rita Mae Brown

"If we could sell our experiences for what they cost us, we'd all be millionaires." Abigail Van Buren

"Experience is the only prophecy of wise men." Alphonse de Lemartine

"You gain strength, courage, and confidence by every experience n which you really stop to look fear in the face. You are able to say to yourself 'I lived through this horror. I can take the next thing that comes along.'" Eleanor Roosevelt

"Experience is not what happens to you; it's what you do with what happens to you." Aldous Huxley

Chapter 88 Expert

"An expert is someone who knows some of the worst mistakes, which can be made, in a very narrow field." Niels Bohr

"An expert is one who knows more and more about less and less." Nicholas Butler

"What's an expert? I read somewhere, that the more a man knows, the more he knows, he doesn't know. So I suppose one definition of an expert would be someone who doesn't admit out loud he knows enough about a subject to know he doesn't really know much." Malcolm S. Forbes

"Always listen to the experts. They'll tell you what can't be done and why. Then do it." Robert Heinlein

"One who limits himself to his chosen mode of ignorance." Elber Hubbard

"We have not overthrown the divine right of kings to fall down for the divine right of experts." Harold Macmillan

"An expert is an ordinary fella away from home." Oail Andrew "Bum" Phillips

"Experts often possess more data than judgment." Colin Powell

"An expert is a person who avoids small errors while sweeping on to the grand fallacy." Steven Weinberger

"There are as many opinions as there are experts." Franklin D. Roosevelt

Chapter 89 Exploration

"Millions of people were inspired by the Apollo Program. I was five years old when I watched Apollo 11 unfold on television, and without any doubt it was a big contributor to my passions for science, engineering, and exploration." Jeff Bezos

"I am very much against weapons in space. And I wish we could be spearheading that program to come to some kind of international agreement so that doesn't happen. That is my only - fear - in further space exploration like always, we hope it doesn't get abused." Scott Bakula

"Exploration is really the essence of the human spirit." Frank Borman

"In wisdom gathered over time I have found that every experience is a form of exploration." Ansel Adams

"The American experience stirred mankind from discovery to exploration. From the cautious quest for what they knew (or thought they knew) was out there, into and enthusiastic reaching to the unknown. These are two substantially different kinds of human enterprise." Daniel J. Boorstin

"We shall not cease from exploration, and the end of all our exploring will be to arrive where we started and know the place for the first time." T.S Eliot

"Emergencies have always been necessary to progress. It was darkness which produced the lamp. It was fog that produced the compass. It was hunger that drove us to exploration. And it took a depression to teach us the real value of a job." Victor Hugo

"Twenty years from now you will be more disappointed by the things you didn't do than by the ones you did do. So throw off the bowlines.

Sail away from the safe harbor. Catch the trade winds in your sails. Explore. Dream. Discover." Mark Twain

"If you wish to advance into the infinite, explore the finite in all directions." Johann Wolfgang von Goethe

"Anyone can look for history in a museum. The creative explorer looks for history in a hardware store." Robert Wieder

Chapter 90 Facts

"Where facts are few, experts are many." Donald R. Gannon

"We can have facts without thinking but we cannot have thinking without facts." John Dewey

"Generally the theories we believe we call facts, and the facts we disbelieve we call theories." Felix Cohen

"Prejudice is a great time saver. You can form opinions without having to get the facts." E. B. White

"The main part of intellectual education is not the acquisition of facts but learning how to make facts live." Oliver Wendell Holmes

"Anyone who says businessmen deal in facts, not fiction, has never read old five-year projections." Malcolm Forbes

"The world is the totality of facts, not of things." Ludwig Wittgenstein

"Science is built up of facts, as a house is with stones. But a collection of facts is no more a science than a heap of stones is a house." Henri Poincare

"The construction of life is at present in the power of facts far more than convictions." Walter Benjamin

"Our best teachers do more than impart facts and figures - they inspire and encourage students and instill a true desire to learn. That's a fine art in itself." Sonny Perdue

Chapter 91 Failure

"Act as if it were impossible to fail." Dorothea Brande

"I can't give you a sure-fire formula for success, but I can give you a formula for failure: try to please everybody all the time." Herbert Bayard Swope

"Don't be discouraged by a failure. It can be a positive experience. Failure is, in a sense, the highway to success, inasmuch as every discovery of what is false leads us to seek earnestly after what is true, and every fresh experience points out some form of error which we shall afterwards carefully avoid." John Keats

"If you have made mistakes, even serious ones, there is always another chance for you. What we call failure is not the falling down but the staying down." Mary Pickford

"Success is the ability to go from one failure to another with no loss of enthusiasm." Sir Winston Churchill

"Many of life's failures are people who did not realize how close they were to success when they gave up." Thomas A. Edison

"I didn't fail the test, I just found 100 ways to do it wrong" Benjamin Franklin

"Good people are good because they've come to wisdom through failure. We get very little wisdom from success, you know." William Saroyan

"An inventor fails 999 times, and if he succeeds once, he's in. He treats his failures simply as practice shots." Charles F. Kettering

"Remember the two benefits of failure. First, if you do fail, you learn what doesn't work; and second, the failure gives you the opportunity to try a new approach." Roger Von Oech

Chapter 92 Faith

"Scepticism is the beginning of Faith." Oscar Wilde

"You block your dream when you allow your fear to grow bigger than your faith." Mary Manin Morrissey

"Faith is a knowledge within the heart, beyond the reach of proof." Kahlil Gibran

"Faith is taking the first step even when you don't see the whole staircase." Martin Luther King, Jr.

"Faith... Must be enforced by reason...When faith becomes blind it dies." Mahatma Gandhi

"The smallest seed of faith is better than the largest fruit of happiness." Henry David Thoreau

"Faith is the daring of the soul to go farther than it can see" William Newton Clarke

"Faith is not belief. Belief is passive. Faith is active." Edith Hamilton

"Faith is a process of leaping into the abyss not on the basis of any certainty about ~where~ we shall land, but rather on the belief that we ~shall~ land." Carter Heyward

"Faith is the strength by which a shattered world shall emerge into the light." Helen Keller

Chapter 93 Fame

**"He who pursues fame at the risk of losing his self is not a scholar."
Chuang-tzu**

"I think the promise of fame and what it holds to you as a child and dreaming of it is not what it is. What it is, I'm not complaining about, but it's just different than the reality you dreamed." Rosie O'Donnell

"Rather than love, than money, than fame, give me truth." Henry David Thoreau

"If you come to fame not understanding who you are, it will define who you are." Oprah Winfrey

"Fame is the thirst of youth." Lord Byron

"All is ephemeral, - fame and the famous as well" Marcus Aurelius

"The highest form of vanity is love of fame." George Santayana

"Fame and tranquility can never be bedfellows." Michel de Montaigne

"Fame is like a shaved pig with a greased tail, and it is only after it has slipped through the hands of some thousands, that some fellow, by mere chance, holds on to it!" Davy Crockett

"I handle fame by not being famous...I'm not famous to me." Bob Marley

Chapter 94 Family

"Rejoice with your family in the beautiful land of life!" Albert Einstein

"When you look at your life, the greatest happinesses are family happinesses." Joyce Brothers

"You don't choose your family. They are God's gift to you, as you are to them." Desmond Tutu

"The family is one of nature's masterpieces." George Santayana

"The only rock I know that stays steady, the only institution I know that works, is the family." Lee Iacocca

"My health and my family are the core of my being." Jon Bon Jovi

"It's really all about family, love and the children for me. I work at that every day." Celine Dion

"The family teaches us about the importance of knowledge, education, hard work and effort. It teaches us about enjoying ourselves, having fun, keeping fit and healthy." Kamisese Mara

"Everybody's family has problems." Greg Kinnear

"We don't have the luxury of time. We spend more because of how we live, but it's important to be with our family and friends." Sara Blakely

Chapter 95 Fashion

"Fashion is a form of ugliness so intolerable that we have to alter it every six months." Oscar Wilde

"Fashions fade, style is eternal." Yves Saint Laurent

"The difference between style and fashion is quality." Giorgio Armani

"It is fancy rather than taste which produces so many new fashions" Voltaire

"As to matters of dress, I would recommend one never to be first in the fashion nor the last out of it" John Wesley

"There is no fashion for the old." Coco Chanel

"Fashion is a social agreement. the result of a consensus of a large group of people." Stella Blum

"Fashion condemns us to many follies; the greatest is to make ourselves its slave" Napoleon Bonaparte

"What a deformed thief this fashion is" William Shakespeare

"There's never a new fashion but it's old." Geoffrey Chaucer

Chapter 96 Fate

"Each man is the architect of his own fate." Appius Claudius

"Fate is nothing but the deeds committed in a prior state of existence." Ralph Waldo Emerson

"Fate is not an eagle, it creeps like a rat." Elizabeth Bowen

"Man does not control his own fate. The women in his life do that for him." Groucho Marx

"Fate determines many things, no matter how we struggle." Otto Weininger

"It is usually more important how a man meets his fate than what it is." Karl Wilhelm Von Humboldt

"There is but one philosophy and its name is fortitude! To bear is to conquer our fate." Edward G. Bulwer-Lytton

"We make our fortunes and we call them fate." Benjamin Disraeli

"Whatever limits us we call fate." Ralph Waldo Emerson

"When an inner situation is not made conscious, it appears outside as fate." Carl Jung

Chapter 97 Fear

"Fear is the tax that conscience pays to guilt." George Sewell

"Fear is a question: What are you afraid of, and why? Just as the seed of health is in illness, because illness contains information, your fears are a treasure house of self-knowledge if you explore them." Marilyn Ferguson

"Feel the fear and do it anyway." Susan Jeffers

"Do not fear mistakes. You will know failure. Continue to reach out." Benjamin Franklin

"Do the thing you fear most and the death of fear is certain." Mark Twain

"He who is not everyday conquering some fear has not learned the secret of life." Ralph Waldo Emerson

"To conquer fear is the beginning of wisdom." Bertrand Russell

"Fear doesn't exist anywhere except in the mind." Dale Carnegie

"Love is what we were born with. Fear is what we learned here." Marianne Williamson

"The meaning I picked, the one that changed my life: Overcome fear, behold wonder." Richard Bach

Chapter 98 Food

"Eat breakfast like a king, lunch like a prince, and dinner like a pauper." Adelle Davis

"Preach not to others what they should eat, but eat as becomes you, and be silent." Epictetus

"If more of us valued food and cheer and song above hoarded gold, it would be a merrier world." J. R. R. Tolkien

"My doctor told me to stop having intimate dinners for four. Unless there are three other people." Orson Welles

"Food is the most primitive form of comfort." Sheila Graham

"Thou shouldst eat to live; not live to eat." Socrates

"Animals are my friends... and I don't eat my friends." George Bernard Shaw

"More die in the United States of too much food than of too little." John Kenneth Galbraith

"Every major food company now has an organic division. There's more capital going into organic agriculture than ever before." Michael Pollan

"Too many people just eat to consume calories. Try dining for a change." John Walters

Chapter 99 Love

"Love is composed of a single soul inhabiting two bodies." Aristotle

"Where there is love there is life." Mahatma Gandhi

"Love is always bestowed as a gift – freely, willingly and without expectation. We don't love to be loved; we love to love." Leo Buscaglia

"Love is an irresistible desire to be irresistibly desired." Robert Frost

"Love is the beauty of the soul." Saint Augustine

"To love oneself is the beginning of a lifelong romance." Oscar Wilde

"Love is the only sane and satisfactory answer to the problem of human existence." Erich Fromm

"Love is a friendship set to music." Joseph Campbell

"Love takes up where knowledge leaves off" Thomas Aquinas

"Don't aim for success if you want it; just do what you love and believe in and it will come naturally." David Frost

Chapter 100 Luck

"Luck is believing you're lucky." Tennessee Williams

"Luck affects everything; let your hook always be cast; in the stream where you least expect it, there will be a fish." Ovid

"Luck is a matter of preparation meeting opportunity." Oprah Winfrey

"Nature creates ability; luck provides it with opportunity." Francois del la Rochefoucauld

"Luck is the tenacity of purpose." Elbert Hubbard

"Being deeply learned and skilled, being well trained and using well spoken words; This is good luck." Buddha

"Nothing is as obnoxious as other people's luck." F. Scott Fitzgerald

"Luck is the residue of design." Branch Rickey

"To a brave man, good and bad luck are like his right and left hand. He uses both." St. Catherine of Siena

"Luck is a dividend of sweat. The more you sweat, the luckier you get." Ray Kroc

Chapter 101 Mankind

"The doctor sees all the weakness of mankind; the lawyer all the wickedness, the theologian all the stupidity." Arthur Schopenhauer

"All that mankind has done, thought or been: it is lying as in magic preservation in the pages of books." Thomas Carlyle

"All the eyes are opened or are opening in the rights of man. The general spread of the light of science has already laid open to every view the palpable truth that the mass of mankind has not been born with saddles on their backs, nor a favoured few booted and spurred ready to ride them legitimately by the grace of God." Thomas Jefferson

"An inability to stay quiet is one of the conspicuous failings of mankind." Walter Bagehot

"And reason... teaches all mankind who will but consult it, that being all equal and independent, no one ought to harm another in his life, health, liberty, or possessions." John Locke

"As I know more of mankind I expect less of them, and am ready now to call a man a good man upon easier terms than I was formerly." Samuel Johnson

"For if the proper study of mankind is man, it is evidently more sensible to occupy yourself with the coherent, substantial and significant creatures of fiction than with the irrational and shadowy figures of her real life." W. Somerset Maugham

"Here men from the planet Earth first set foot upon the Moon. July 1969 AD. We came in peace for all mankind." Neil Armstrong

"I don't resist progress, but I have a growing feeling that mankind uses it mostly for disgraceful purposes." Stanislaw J. Lem

"I have offended God and mankind because my work didn't reach the quality it should have." Leonardo da Vinci

"If all mankind minus one were of one opinion, and only one person were of the contrary opinion, mankind would be no more justified in silencing that one person than he, if he had the power, would be justified in silencing mankind." John Stuart Mill

Chapter 102 Marriage

"Strike an average between what a woman thinks of her husband a month before she marries him and what she thinks of him a year afterward, and you will have the truth about him" H.L. Mencken

"More marriages might survive if the partners realized that sometimes the better comes after the worse." Doug Larson

"Many a man in love with a dimple makes the mistake of marrying the whole girl." Stephen Leacock

"A dog is much like a married man, obeying his master's voice for the sake of his master's touch." Robert Brault

"Marriage is a mistake every man should make." George Jessel

"Love is blind, but marriage restores its sight." Samuel Lichtenberg

"When a man opens the car door for his wife, it's either a new car or a new wife." Prince Philip

"Why does a woman work ten years to change a man's habits and then complain that he's not the man she married." Barbra Streisand

"Marriage does not unite two people; it entangles them." Abraham Miller

"The bonds of matrimony are like any other bonds – they mature slowly." Peter De Vries

Chapter 103 Mathematics

"If people do not believe that mathematics is simple, it is only because they do not realize how complicated life is." John Louis von Neumann

"Pure mathematics is , in its way, the poetry of logical ideas." Albert Einstein

"The essence of mathematics is not to make simple things complicated, but to make complicated things simple." S. Gudder

"If there is a God, he's a great mathematician." Paul Dirac

"Pure mathematics is the world's best game. It is more absorbing than chess, more of a gamble than poker, and lasts longer than Monopoly. It's free. It can be played anywhere – Archimedes did it in a bathtub." Richard J. Trudeau

"The man ignorant of mathematics will be increasingly limited in his grasp of the main forces of civilization." John Kemeny

"The definition of a good mathematical problem is the mathematics it generates rather than the problem itself." Andrew Wiles

"Mathematics is a game played according to certain simple rules with meaningless marks on paper." David Hilbert

"It is hard to know what you are talking about in mathematics, yet no one questions the validity of what you say. There is no other realm of discourse so queer." James Newman

"Mathematics is the most beautiful and most powerful creation of the human spirit." Stefan Banach

Chapter 104 Maturity

"Maturity is a bitter disappointment for which no remedy exists, unless laughter could be said to remedy anything." Kurt Vonnegut

"Maturity is achieved when a person accepts life as full of tension." Joshua L. Liebman

"A mature person is one who does not think in absolutes, who is able to be objective even when deeply stirred emotionally, who has learned that there is both good and bad in all people and all things, and who walks humbly and charitably." Eleanor Roosevelt

"Maturity is: The ability to stick with a job until it's finished. The ability to do a job without being supervised; The ability to carry money without spending it; and the ability to bear an injustice without wanting to get even." Abigail Van Buren

"To make mistakes is human; to stumble is commonplace; to be able to laugh at yourself is maturity." William Arthur Ward

"Maturity is the ability to think, speak and act your feelings within the bounds of dignity. The measure of your maturity is how spiritual you become during the midst of your frustrations." Samuel Ullman

"Maturity is a high price to pay for growing up." Tom Stoppard

"'Age' is the acceptance of a term of years. But maturity is the glory of the years." Martha Graham

"Maturity is the capacity to endure uncertainty." John Huston Finley

"One sign of maturity is the ability to be comfortable with people who are not like us." Virgil A. Kraft

Chapter 105 Medicine

"Our food should be our medicine and our medicine should be our food." Hippocrates

"Walking is man's best medicine." Hippocrates

"Medicine, the only profession that labors incessantly to destroy the reason for its existence." James Bryce

"Make hunger thy sauce, as a medicine for health." Thomas Tusser

"A vigorous five-mile walk will do more good for an unhappy but otherwise healthy adult than all the medicine and psychology in the world." Paul Dudley

"The practice of medicine is a thinker's art the practice of surgery a plumber's." Martin H. Fischer

"The aim of medicine is to prevent disease and prolong life, the ideal of medicine is to eliminate the need for a physician." William J. Mayo

"One-quarter of what you eat keeps you alive. The other three-quarters keeps your doctor alive." (Hieroglyph found in an ancient Egyptian tomb.)

"I find medicine is the best of all trades because whether you do any good or not you still get your money." Moliere

"But if you're asking my opinion, I would argue that a social justice approach should be central to medicine and utilized to be central to public health. This could be very simple: the well should take care of the sick." Paul Farmer

Chapter 106 Memory

"Reminscences make one feel so deliciously aged and sad." George Bernard Shaw

 "The more you love a memory, the stronger and stranger it is." Vladimir Nabokov

"If we lose our memory, we lose ourselves Forgetting is one of the symptoms of death. Without memory we cease to be human beings." Ivan Klima

"Memory is the scribe of the soul." Aristotle

"Memory is the cabinet of imagination, the treasury of reason, the registry of the conscience, and, the council chamber of thought." Basile

"Like ultraviolet rays memory shows to each man in the book of life a script that invisibly and prophetically glosses the text." Walter Benjamin

"The more connections that can be made in the brain, the more integrated the experience is within the memory." Don Campbell

"Memory is the greatest of artists, and effaces from your mind what is unnecessary." Maurice Baring

"Every man's memory is his private literature." Aldous Huxley

"A good memory is needed after one has lied." Pierre Corneille

Chapter 107 Men and Women

"Most of us women like men, you know; it's just that we find them a constant disappointment." Clare Short

"Only one man in a thousand is a leader of men, the other 999 follow women." Groucho Marx

"Waste no more time arguing about what a good man should be. Be one." Marcus Aurelius

"You see a lot of smart guys with dumb women, but you hardly ever see a smart woman with a dumb guy." Erica Jong

"When he's late for dinner, I know he's either having an affair or is lying dead in the street. I always hope it's the street." Jessica Tandy

"After a few years of marriage a man can look right at a woman without seeing her and a woman can see right through a man without looking at him." Helen Rowland

"As usual, there is a great woman behind every idiot." John Lennon

"Woman was God's second mistake." Friedrich Nietzsche

"Once a woman has a forgiven a man, she must not reheat his sins from breakfast." Marlene Dietrich

"There is nothing like a good dose of another woman to make a man appreciate his wife." Clare Booth Luce

"Happiness? A good cigar, a good meal, a good cigar and a good woman – or a bad woman; it depends on how much happiness you can handle." George Burns

Chapter 108 Mercy

"I have always found that mercy bears richer fruits than strict justice."
Abraham Lincoln

"Think carefully before asking for justice. Mercy might be safer."
Mason Cooley

"We hand folks over to God's mercy and show none ourselves."
George Eliot

"The very contradictions in my life are in some ways signs of God's mercy to me." Thomas Merton

"Cowards are cruel, but the brave love mercy and delight to save." John Gay

"A man gazing on the stars is proverbially at the mercy of the puddles in the road." Alexander Smith

"I suspect that even today, with all the progress we have made in liberal thought, the quality of true tolerance is as rare as the quality of mercy." Frank Knox

"Mercy to animals means mercy to mankind." Henry Bergh

"Computers are like Old Testament gods; lots of rules and no mercy." Joesph Campbell

"The most valuable things in life are not measured in monetary terms. The really important things are not houses and lands, stocks and bonds, automobiles and real estate, but friendships, trust, confidence, empathy, mercy, love and faith." Bertrand Russell

Chapter 109 Mistakes

"A life spent making mistakes is not only more honorable, but more useful than a life spent doing nothing." George Bernard Shaw

"A man must be big enough to admit his mistakes, smart enough to profit from them, and strong enough to correct them." John C. Maxwell

"Do not fear mistakes. You will know failure. Continue to reach out." Benjamin Franklin

"Sometimes when you innovate, you make mistakes. It is best to admit them quickly, and get on with improving your other innovations." Steve Jobs

"Feelings of worth can flourish only in an atmosphere where individual differences are appreciated, mistakes are tolerated, communication is open, and rules are flexible – the kind of atmosphere that is found in a nurturing family." Virginia Satir

"Forgive yourself for your faults and your mistakes and move on."Les Brown

"Success does not consist in never making mistakes but in never making the same one a second time." George Bernard Shaw

"Mistakes are almost always of a sacred nature. Never try to correct them. On the contrary: rationalize them, understand them thoroughly. After that, it will be possible for you to sublimate them." Salvador Dali

"A doctor can bury his mistakes but an architect can only advise his clients to plant vines." Frank Lloyd Wright

"Even the knowledge of my own fallibility cannot keep me from making mistakes. Only when I fall do I get up again." Vincent Van Gogh

Chapter 110 Money

"A little thought and a little kindness are often worth more than a great deal of money." John Ruskin

"When I was young I thought that money was the most important thing in life; now that I am old I know that it is." Oscar Wilde

"Honesty is the best policy – when there is money in it." Mark Twain

"Money: power is at its most liquid." Mason Cooley

"Money is better than poverty, if only for financial reasons." Woody Allen

"A good reputation is more valuable than money." Publilius Syrus

"It is more rewarding to watch money change the world than watch it accumulate." Gloria Steinem

"Sooner or later, we all sell out for money." Tony Randall

"A nation that continues year after year to spend more money on military defense than on programs of social uplift is approaching spiritual doom." Martin Luther King, Jr.

"Rule No.1: Never lose money. Rule No.2: Never forget rule No. 1." Warren Buffett

Chapter 111 Morality

"Aim above morality. Be not simply good, be good for something."
Henry David Thoreau

"Force always attacts men of low morality." Albert Einstein

"Truth is certainly a branch of morality and a very important one to society." Thomas Jefferson

"Compassion is the basis of morality." Arthur Schopenhauer

"Morality is contraband in war." Mahatma Gandhi

"I think the greater responsibility, in terms of morality, is where leadership begins." Norman Lear

"Money motivates neither the best people, nor the best in people. It can move the body and influence the mind, but it cannot touch the heart or move the spirit; that is reserved for belief, principle, and morality." Dee Hock

"Respect for the truth comes close to being the basis for all morality." Frank Herbert

"When morality comes up against, it is seldom profit that loses." Shirley Chisholm

"Morality may consist solely in the courage of making a choice." Leon Blum

Chapter 112 Music

"Music is enough for a lifetime, but a lifetime is not enough for music." Sergei Rachmaninov

"Music expresses that which cannot be put into words and cannot remain silent." Victor Hugo

"Words make you think a thought. Music makes you feel a feeling. A song makes you feel a thought." E. Y. Harburg

"Music fills the infinite between two souls." Rabindranath Tagore

"If a man does not keep pace with the companions, perhaps it is because he hears a different drummer. Let him step to the music which he hears, however measured or far away." Henry David Thoreau

"Without music, life would be an error." Friedrich Nietzsche

"Music is an outburst of the soul." Frederick Delius

"Music the art of thinking with sounds." Jules Combarieu

"Music is perpetual, and only the hearing is intermittent." Henry David Thoreau

"Where words fail, music speaks." Hans Christian Andersen

Chapter 113 Nature

"How strange that Nature does not knock, and yet does not intrude!" Emily Dickinson

"How glorious a greeting the sun gives the mountains!" John Muir

"Adopt the pace of nature; her secret is patience." Ralph Waldo Emerson

"I believe that there is a subtle magnetism in Nature, which if we unconsciously yield to it, will direct us aright." Henry David Thoreau

"Forget not that the earth delights to feel your bare feet and the winds long to play with your hair." Kahlil Gibran

"Everybody needs beauty as well as bread, places to play in and pray in, where nature may heal and give strength to body and soul." John Muir

"The poetry of the earth is never dead." John Keats

"Nature does not hurry, yet everything is accomplished." Lao Tzu

"One touch of nature makes the whole world kin." William Shakespeare

"If you truly love Nature, you will find beauty everywhere." Vincent Van Gogh

Chapter 114 Necessity

"Necessity is the mother of taking chances." Mark Twain

"Discontent is the first necessity of progress." Thomas A. Edison

"Work is a necessity for man. Man invented the alarm clock." Pablo Picasso

"Nothing would be more tiresome than eating and drinking if God had not made them a pleasure as well as a necessity." Voltaire

"Necessity makes even the timid brave." Sallust

"Our soul is cast into a body, where it finds number, time, dimension. Thereupon it reasons and calls this nature necessity, and can belive nothing else." Blaise Pascal

"It is necessary to posit something which is necessary of itself, and has no cause of its necessity outside of itself but is the cause of necessity in other things. And all people call this thing God." Thomas Aquinas

"Nothing has more strength than dire necessity." Euripides

"To doubt everything, or, to believe everything, are two equally convenient solutions; both dispense with the necessity of reflection." Henri Poincare

"Everything existing in the universe is the fruit of chance and necessity." Democritus

Chapter 115 Nobility

"They are never alone that are accompanied with noble thoughts." Sir Philip Sidney

"A noble person noble people, and knows how to hold on to them." Johann Wolfgang von Goethe

"True nobility is exempt from fear." Marcus Tullius Cicero

"Be noble! And the nobleness that lies in other men, sleeping , but never dead, will rise in majesty to meet thine own." James Russell Lowell

"If there is anything good about nobility it is that it enforces the necessity of avoiding degeneracy." Boethius

"Nobility is a river that sets with a constant and undeviating current, directly into the great Pacific Ocean of Time; but, unlike all other rivers, it is more grand at its source, than at its termination." Charles Calob Colton

"Put more trust in nobility of character than in an oath." Solon

"Nobility of spirit has more to do with simplicity than ostentation, wisdom rather than wealth, commitment rather than ambition." Riccardo Muti

"The noblest heart is stained by the addition of pride." Claudian

"There is in the worst of fortune the best of chances for a happy change." Euripedes

"A noble heart cannot suspect in others the pettiness and malice that it has never felt." Jean Racine

Chapter 116 Opinions

"I think we ought always to entertain our opinions with some measure of doubt. I shouldn't wish people dogmatically to believe any philosophy, not even mine." Bertrand Russell

"Fight for your opinions, but do not believe they contain the whole truth, or the only truth." Charles A. Dana

"The recipe for perpetual ignorance is: be satisfied with your opinions and content with your knowledge." Elbert Hubbard

"Nothing is more conducive to peace of mind than not having any opinions at all." Georg Chrisoph Lichtenberg

"There is no greater mistake than the hasty conclusion that opinions are worthless because they are badly argued." Thomas H. Huxley

"Where there is much desire to learn, there of necessity will be much arguing, much writing, many opinions; for opinion in good men is but knowledge in the making." John Milton

"Ten gods cannot change the opinion of one fool, especially if another fool agrees with him." Abraham Miller

"There is nothing in the world so easy as giving an opinion; consequently, in general, there are few things so utterly valueless." Charles William Day

"I never submitted the whole system of my opinions to the creed of any party of men whatever, in religion, in philosophy, in politics, or in anything else, where I was capable of thinking for myself. Such an addiction is the last degradation of a free and moral agent. If I could not go to heaven but with a party, I would not go there at all." Thomas Jefferson

"Your opinion is your opinion, your perception is your perception—do not confuse them with "facts" or "truth". Wars have been fought and millions have been killed because of the inability of men to understand the idea that EVERYBODY has a different viewpoint." John Muir

Chapter 117 Opportunity

"We are all faced with a series of great opportunities brilliantly disguised as impossible situations." Charles R. Swindoll

"Don't wait for extraordinary opportunities. Seize the common occasions and make them great. Weak men wait for opportunities; strong men make them." Orison Swett Marden

"It is the responsibility of leadership to provide opportunity, and the responsibility of individuals to contribute." William Pollard

"He who refuses to embrace a unique opportunity loses the prize as surely as if he had failed." William James

"Opportunities to find deeper powers within ourselves come when life seems most challenging." Joseph Campbell

"Most successful men have not achieved their distinction by having some new talent or opportunity presented to them. They have developed the opportunity that was at hand." Bruce Marton

"Every day is a new opportunity. You can build on yesterday's success or put its failures behind and start over again. That's the way life is, with a new game every day, and that's the way baseball is." Bob Feller

"When written in Chinese, the word 'crisis' is composed of two characters- one represents danger, and the other represents opportunity." John Fitzgerald Kennedy

"Problems can become opportunities when the right people come together." Robert South

"To improve the golden amount of opportunity, and catch the good that is within our reach, is the great art of life." Samuel Johnson

Chapter 118 Optimism

"Optimism is the faith that leads to achievement. Nothing can be done without hope and confidence." Helen Keller

"The basis of optimism is sheer terror." Oscar Wilde

"Optimism is a kind of heart stimulant- the digitalis of failure." Elbert Hubbard

"There is only one optimist. He has been here since man has been on this earth, and that is man himself. If we hadn't had such a magnificient optimism to carry us through all these things, we wouldn't be here. We have survived it on our optimism." Edward Steichen

"A pessimist sees the difficulty in every opportunity; an optimist sees the opportunity in every difficulty." Winston Churchill

"The pessimist complains about the wind; the optimist expects it to change; the realist adjusts the sails." William Arthur Ward

"Optimist: Day-dreamer more elegantly spelled." Mark Twain

"The man who is a pessimist before forty-eight knows too much; if he is an optimist after it he knows too little." Mark Twain

"An optimist is the human personification of spring." Susan J. Bissonette

"In the long run the pessimist may be proved right, but the optimist has a better time on the trip." Daniel L. Reardon

Chapter 119 Painting

"A painting in a museum hears more ridiculous opinions than anything else in the world" Edmond de Goncourt

"Every artist dips his brush in his own soul, and paints his own nature into his pictures." Henry Ward Beecher

"A man paints with his brains and not with his hands." Michelangelo Buonarroti

"Painting is a silent poetry, and poetry is painting with the gift of speech." Simonides

"Only when he no longer knows what he is doing does the painter do good things." Edgar Degas

"I experience a period of frightening clarity in those moments when nature is so beautiful. I am no longer size of myself, and the paintings appear as in a dream." Vincent van Gogh

"I've been a lot of abstract painting lately, extremely abstract. No brush, no paint, no canvas, I just think about it." Stephen Wright

"Painting is easy when you don't know how, but very difficult when you do." Edgar Degas

"I don't paint things. I only paint the difference between things." Henri Matisse

"If no one ever took risks, MIchaelangelo would have painted the Sistine floor." Neil Simon

Chapter 120 Parents

"Just a word of advice. Whenever you're furious with your parents or you think they're terrible, just remember, you vomited on them and they kept you." John Green

"You don't really understand human nature unless you know why a child on a merry-go-round will wave at his parents every time around – and why his parents will always wave back." William D. Tammeus

"Before I got married I had six theories about bringing up children; now I have six children and no theories." John Wilmot

"Don't worry that children never listen to you; worry that they are always watching you." Robert Fulgham

"There are two lasting bequests we can give our children. One is roots. The other is wings." Hodding Carter, Jr.

"Do not ask that your kids live up to your expectations. Let your kids be who they are, and your expectations will be in breathless pursuit." Robert Brault

"Let parents bequeath to their children not riches, but the spirit of reverence." Plato

"The truth is that parents are not really interested in justice. They just want quiet." Bill Cosby

"As you get older you have more respect and empathy for your parents. Now I have a great relationship with both of them." Hugh Jackman

"The child supplies the power but the parents have to do the steering." Benjamin Spock

Chapter 121 Passion

"Only passions, great passions, can elevate the soul to great things."
Denis Diderot

"You will need to find your passion. Don't give up on finding it because then all you're doing is waiting for the Reaper." Randy Pausch

"It's the soul's duty to be loyal to its own desires. It must abandon itself to its master passion." Rebecca West

"Nothing great in the world has ever been accomplished without passion." Hebbel

"A great leader's courage to fulfill his vision comes from passion, not position." John Maxwell

"A strong passion for any object will ensure success, for the desire of the end will point out the means." William Hazlin

"There is no end. There is no beginning. There is only the passion of life." Federico Fellini

"Develop a passion for learning. If you do, you will never cease to grow." Anthony D'Angelo

"Rest in reason; move in passion." Khalil Gibran

"Passion is the genius of genius." Anthony Robbins

Chapter 122 Patience

"Patience is the greatest of all virtues." Cato the Elder

"The fates have given mankind a patient soul." Homer

"Patience serves as a protection against wrongs as clothes do against cold. For if you put on more clothes as the cold increases, it will have no power to hurt you. So in like manner you must grow in patience when you meet with great wrongs, and they will then be powerless to vex your mind." Leonardo da Vinci

"Patience is the companion of wisdom." Saint Augustine

"Patience and fortitude conquer all things." Ralph Waldo Emerson

"The key to everything is patience. You get the chicken by hatching the egg, not by smashing it." Arnold H. Glasgow

"Patience is bitter but its fruit is sweet." Jean-Jacques Rousseau

"Patience is not passive; on the contrary it is active; it is concentrated strength." Edward G. Bulwer-Lytton

"Patience is the most necessary quality for business, many a man would rather you heard his story than grant his request." Lord Chesterfield

"As you put into practice the qualities of patience, punctuality, sincerity, and solicitude, you will have a better opinion of the world around you." Grenville Kleiser

"Endurance is the crowning quality. And patience all the passion of great hearts." James Russell Lowell

Chapter 123 Patriotism

"Our obligation to our country never cease but with our lives." John Adams

"'My country, right or wrong,' is a thing that no patriot would think of saying except in a desperate case. It is like saying 'My mother, drunk or sober.' " G.K Chesterton

"Patriotism is supporting your country all the time, and your government when it deserves it." Mark Twain

"If I had to choose between betraying my country and betraying my friend, I hope I should have the guts to betray my country." E.M Forster

"The highest form of patriotism is not a blind acceptance of official policy, but a love of one's country deep enough to call her to a higher plain." George McGovern

"Patriotism is not short, frenzied outbursts of emotion, but the tranquil and steady dedication of a lifetime." Adlai E. Stevenson

"Patriotism means unqualified and unwavering love for the nation, which implies not uncritical eagerness to serve, not support for unjust claims, but frank assessment of its vices and sins, and penitence for them." Alexander Solzhenitsyn

"Patriotism is one of the unalterable facts of man's nature. It is a virtue if you like it, and a vice if you don't like it." Max Eastman

"When a whole nation is roaring patriotism at the top of its voice, I am fain to explore the cleanness of its hands and the purity of its heart." Ralph Waldo Emerson

"Those who love their country never wish to rule it." Abraham Miller

Chapter 124 Peace

"If you want to make peace, you don't talk to your friends. You talk to your enemies." Moshe Dayan

"If we have no peace, it is because we have forgotten that we belong each other." Mother Theresa

"Yes, we love peace, but we are not willing to take wounds for it, as we are for war." John Andrew Holmes

"A warless world will come as men develop warless hearts." Charles Wesley Burns

"One day we must come to see that peace is not merely a distant goal that we seek, but that it is a means by which we arrive at that goal. We must pursue peaceful ends through peaceful means." Reverend Dr. Martin Luther King, Jr.

"Peace cannot be achieved through violence, it can only be attained through understanding." Ralph Waldo Emerson

"Peace comes from within. Do not seek it without." Buddha

"Peace is its own reward." Mahatma Gandhi

"Peace is the only battle worth waging." Albert Camus

"Peace can only last where human rights are respected, where the people are fed, and where individuals and nations are free." Dalai Lama

Chapter 125 Perfection

"Perfection is a road, not a destination. Every time I live, I get an education." Burk Hudson

"The idea of perfect closes your mind to new standards. When you drive hard toward one ideal, you miss opportunities and paths, not to mention hurting your confidence. Believe in your potential and then go out and explore it; don't limit it." John Eliot, Ph.D

"I am careful not to confuse excellence with perfection. Excellence, I can reach for; perfection is God's business." Michael J. Fox

"They say that nobody is perfect. Then they tell you practice makes perfect. I wish they'd make up their minds." Winston Churchill

"Perfection is attained by slow degrees; it requires the hand of time." Voltaire

"People throw away what they could have by insisting on perfection, which they cannot have, and looking for it where they will never find it." Edith Schaeffer

"Perfection is slow death." Hugh Prather

"Aim at perfection in everything, though in most things it is unattainable. However, they who aim it, and persevere, will come much nearer to it than those whose laziness and despondency make them give it up as unattainable." Lord Chesterfield

"Perfectionism is the enemy of creation, as extreme self-solitude is the enemy of the well-being." John Updike

"Done is better than perfect." Scott Allen

Chapter 126 Perseverance

**"Great works are performed not by strength but by perseverance."
Samuel Johnson**

"Men fail much oftener from want to perseverance than from want of talent." William Cobbett

"In the confrontation between the stream and the rock, the stream wins – not through strength but by perseverance." H. Jackson Brown

"One of the commonest mistakes and one of the costliest is thinking that success is due to some genius, some magic – something or other which we do not possess. Success is generally due to holding on, and failure to letting go. You decide to learn a language, study music, take a course reading, train yourself physically. Will it be success or failure? It depends upon how much pluck and perseverance that word "decide" contains. The decision that nothing can overrule, the grip that nothing can detach will bring success. Remember the Chinese proverb, 'With time and patience, the mulberry leaf becomes satin'." Maltbie Davenport Babcock

"Perseverance is not a long race; it is many short races one after another." Walter Elliott

"The miracle, or the power, that elevates the few is to be found in their industry, application, and perseverance under the promptings of a brave, determined spirit." Mark Twain

"Genius is divine perseverance. Genius I cannot claim nor even extra brightness but perseverance all can have." Woodrow Wilson

"Thankfully, perseverance is a good substitute for talent." Steve Martin

"Permanence, perseverance and persistence in spite of all obstacles, discouragements and impossibilities: It is this, that in all things distinguishes the strong soul from the weak." Thomas Carlyle

"The most interesting about a postage stamp is the persistence with which it sticks to its job." Napoleon Hill

Chapter 127 Persistence

"A little more persistence, a little more effort, and what seemed hopeless failure may turn to glorious success." Elbert Hubbard

"Persistence is to the character of man as carbon is to steel." Napoleon Hill

"The difference between people who believe they have books inside of them and those who actually write books is sheer cussed persistence – the ability to make yourself work at your craft, every day – the belief, even in the face of obstacles, that you've got something worth saying." Jennifer Warner

"To make our way, we must have firm resolve, persistence, tenacity. We must gear ourselves to work hard all the way. We can never let up." Ralph Bunche

"The most essential factor is persistence – the determination never to allow your energy or enthusiasm to be dampened by the discouragement that must inevitably come." James Whitcomb Riley

"No great achievement is possible without persistent work." Bertrand Russell

"Making your mark on the world is hard. If it were easy, everybody would do it. But it's not. It takes patience, it takes commitment, and it comes with plenty of failure along the way. The real test is not whether you avoid this failure, because you won't. It's whether you let it harden or shame you into inaction, or whether you learn from it; whether you choose to persevere." Barack Obama

"Success is stumbling from failure to failure with no loss of enthusiasm." Winston Churchill

"Knowing trees, I understand the meaning of patience. Knowing grass, I can appreciate persistence." Hal Borland

"As long as there's breath in you- PERSIST!" Bernard Kelvin Clive

Chapter 128 Pets

"We call them dumb animals, and so they are, for they cannot tell us how they feel, but they do not suffer less because they have no words." Anna Sewell

"Animals are such agreeable friends – they ask no questions, they pass no criticisms." George Eliot

"The difference between friends and pets is that friends we allow into our company, pets we allow into our solitude." Robert Brault

"Until one has loved an animal, a part of one's soul remains unawakened." Anatole France

"It often happens that a man is more humanely related to a cat or dog than to any human being." Henry David Thoreau

"I have been studying the traits and dispositions of 'lower animals')so called) and contrasting them with traits and dispositions of man." Mark Twain

"To insult someone we call him 'bestial'. For deliberate cruelty and nature, 'human' might be the greater insult." Isaac Asimov

"The worst sin towards our fellow creatures is not to hate them, but to be indifferent to them. That's the essence of inhumanity." George Bernard Shaw

"An animal's eyes have the power to speak a great language." Martin Buber

"Love the animals: God has given them the rudiments of thought and joy untroubled" Fyodor Dostoyevsky

"If you have men who will exclude any of God's creatures from the shelter of compassion and pity, you will have men who will deal likewise with their fellow men." St. Francis of Assisi

Chapter 129 Philosophy

"The point of philosophy is to start with something so simple as not to seem worth stating, and to end with something so paradoxical that no one will believe it." Bertrand Russell

"There is nothing so absurd but some philosopher has said it." Cicero

"Philosophy consists very largely of one philosopher arguing that all others are jackasses. He usually proves it, and I should add that he also usually proves that he is one himself." H. L. Mencken

"Philosophy is a battle against the bewitchment of our intelligence by means of language." Ludwig Wittgenstein

"There is only one thing a philosopher can be relied upon to do, and that is to contradict other philosophers." William James

"When he who hears does not know what he who speaks means, and when he who speaks does not know what he himself means, that is philosophy" Voltaire

"I would not think that philosophy and reason themselves will be man's guide in the foreseeable future; however, they will remain the most beautiful sanctuary they have always been for the select few" Albert Einstein

"Philosophy is an elegant thing, if anyone modestly meddles with it; but if they are conversant with it more than is becoming, it corrupts them." Plato

"To be a philosopher is not merely to have subtle thoughts, nor even to found a school, but to so love wisdom as to live according to its dictates a life of simplicity, independence, magnanimity and trust." Henry David Thoreau

"Philosophy is like trying to open a safe with a combination lock: each little adjustment of the dials seems to achieve nothing, only when everything is in place does the door open." Ludwig Wittgenstein

Chapter 130 Photography

"Sometimes I do get to places just when God's ready to have somebody click the shutter." Ansel Adams

"No place is boring, if you've had a good night's sleep and have a pocket full of unexposed film." Robert Adams

"A good snapshot stops a moment from running away." Eudora Welty

"I'm not a particularly verbose person. I think that's why I like taking pictures... they speak for themselves." Jeb Dickerson

"Photographers deal in things which are continually vanishing and when they have vanished there is no contrivance on earth which can make them come back again." Henri Cartier Bresson

"Photography through the camera is an instrument of detection. We photograph not only what we know, but also what we don't know." Lisette Model

"A photograph is a secret about a secret. The more it tells you the less you know." Diane Arbus

"Photography is the only language that can be understood anywhere in the world." Bruno Barbey

"Taking pictures is like fishing or writing. It's getting out of the unknown that which resists and refuses to come to light" Jean Gaumy

"Photography takes an instant out of time, altering life by holding it still." Dorothea Lange

"I went into photography because it seemed like the perfect vehicle for commenting on the madness of today's existence." Robert Mapplethorpe

Chapter 131 Physics

"Not only is the universe stranger than we imagine, it is stranger than we can imagine." Sir Arthur Eddington

"In the matter of physics, the first lessons should contain nothing but what is experimental and interesting to see. A pretty experiment is in itself often more valuable than twenty formulae extracted from our minds." Albert Einstein

"In physics, you don't have to go around making trouble for yourself - nature does it for you." Frank Wilczek

"It should be possible to explain the laws of physics to a barmaid." Albert Einstein

"If anybody says he can think about quantum physics without getting giddy, that only shows he has not understood the first thing about them." Niels Bohr

"Chemistry has been termed by the physicist as the messy part of physics, but that is no reason why the physicists should be permitted to make a mess of chemistry when they invade it." Frederick Soddy

"It is impossible to trap modern physics into predicting anything with perfect determinism because it deals with probabilities from the outset." Arthur Eddington

"Physics is, hopefully, simple. Physicists are not." Edward Teller

"Physics is becoming so unbelievably complex that it is taking longer and longer to train a physicist. It is taking so long, in fact, to train a physicist to the place where he understands the nature of physical problems that he is already too old to solve them." Eugene Wigner

"Physics isn't a religion. If it were, we'd have a much easier time raising money." Leon Lederman

"I am now convinced that theoretical physics is actually philosophy." Max Born

Chapter 132 Plagiarism

"To steal ideas from one person is plagiarism, to steal ideas from many is research." Wilson Mizner

"The secret to creativity is knowing how to hide your sources." Albert Einstein

"About the most originality that any writer can hope to achieve honestly is to steal with good judgment." Josh Billings

"Art is either plagiarism or revolution." Paul Gauguin

"There is much difference between imitating a man and counterfeiting him." Benjamin Franklin

"Plagiarists at least have the quality of preservation." Benjamin Disraeli

"Genius borrows nobly." Ralph Waldo Emerson

"When a thing has been said and said well, have no scruple. Take it and copy it." Anatole France

"Nothing is said which has not been said before." Terence

"If we steal thoughts from the moderns, it will be cried down as plagiarism; if from the ancients, it will be cried up as erudition" Charles Caleb Colton

Chapter 133 Plans

"Make no little plans; they have no magic to stir men's blood...Make big plans, aim high in hope and work." Daniel H. Burnham

"We must be willing to get rid of the life we've planned, so as to have the life that is waiting for us." Joseph Campbell

"Plans are only good intentions unless they immediately degenerate into hard work." Peter Drucker

"It is a bad plan that admits of no modification." Publilius Syrus

"Expect the best, plan for the worst, and prepare to be surprised." Denis Waitley

"Without leaps of imagination, or dreaming, we lose the excitement of possibilities. Dreaming, after all, is a form of planning." Gloria Steinem

"You can never plan the future by the past." Edmund Burke

"Thinking well to be wise: planning well, wiser: doing well wisest and best of all." Malcolm Forbes

"Meticulous planning will enable everything a man does to appear spontaneous." Mark Caine

Chapter 134 Poetry

"Poetry is just the evidence of life. If your life is burning well, poetry is just the ash." Leonard Cohen

"He who draws noble delights from sentiments of poetry is a true poet, though he has never written a line in all his life." George Sand

"A poem begins with a lump in the throat." Robert Frost

"The true poet is all the time a visionary and whether with friends or not, as much alone as a man on his death bed." W.B. Yeats

"Poetry is the language in which man explores his own amazement." Christopher Fry

"Each man carries within him the soul of a poet who died young." Sainte-Beuve

"God is the perfect poet." Robert Browning

"Poetry is when an emotion has found its thought and the thought has found words." Robert Frost

"A poet is a man who puts up a ladder to a star and climbs it while playing a violin." Edmond de Goncourt

"Poetry is the universal language which the heart holds with nature and itself." William Hazlitt

Chapter 135 Politician

"Under every stone lurks a politician." Aristophanes

"Now I know what a statesman is; he's a dead politician. We need more statesmen." Bob Edwards

"An honest politician is one who, when he is bought, will stay bought." Simon Cameron

"Men say I am a saint losing himself in politics. The fact is that I am a politician trying my hardest to become a saint." Mahatma Gandhi

"Politics: "Poli" a Latin word meaning "many"; and "tics" meaning "bloodsucking creatures"." Robin Williams

"Everything is changing. People are taking their comedians seriously and the politicians as a joke." Will Rogers

"Whoever makes two ears of corn, or two blades of grass to grow where only one grew before, deserves better of mankind, and does more essential service to his country than the whole race of politicians put together" Jonathan Swift

"A good politician is quite as unthinkable as an honest burglar" Henry Louis Mencken

"My choice early in life was either to be a piano-player in a whorehouse or a politician. And to tell the truth, there's hardly any difference." Harry S Truman

Chapter 136 Politics

"Crime does not pay ... as well as politics." Alfred E. Newman

"The whole aim of practical politics is to keep the populace alarmed (and hence clamorous to be led to safety) by menacing it with an endless series of hobgoblins, all of them imaginary." H. L. Mencken

"Politics is the art of looking for trouble, finding it whether it exists or not, diagnosing it incorrectly, and applying the wrong remedy." Ernest Benn

"Politics is the art of preventing people from taking part in affairs which properly concern them." Paul Valery

"The most practical kind of politics is the politics of decency." Theodore Roosevelt

"The whole art of politics consists in directing rationally the irrationalities of men." Reinhold Niebuhr

"If you have sense enough to realize why flies gather around a restaurant, you should be able to appreciate why men run for office." Edgar Watson Howe

"The only motive that can keep politics pure is the motive of doing good for one's country and its people." Henry Ford

"Politics is the art of postponing decisions until they are no longer relevant." Henri Queuille

"Sometimes I wonder if we shall ever grow up in our politics and say definite things which mean something, or whether we shall always go on using generalities to which everyone can subscribe, and which mean very little." Eleanor Roosevelt

Chapter 137 Possessions

"I love stuff as much as the next guy, but I've come to understand that, regardless of the cost of acquiring it, the price of having it is freedom." Colleen Wainwright

"Before we set our hearts too much upon anything, let us examine how happy those are who already possess it." Francois de La Rochefoucauld

"Every increased possession loads us with new weariness." John Ruskin

"To have little is to possess.To have plenty is to be perplexed." Lao-tzu

"An object in possession seldom retains the same charm that it had in pursuit." Pliny the Younger

"What difference does it make how much you have? What you do not have amounts to much more." Seneca

"Nowadays the rage for possession has got to such a pitch that there is nothing in the realm of nature, whether sacred or profane, out of which profit cannot be squeezed" Desiderius Erasmus

"A man's real possession is his memory. In nothing else is he rich, in nothing else is he poor." Alexander Smith

"It is preoccupation with possession, more than anything else, that prevents men from living freely and nobly" Bertrand Russell

"Possession diminishes perception of value, immediately" John Updike

Chapter 138 Poverty

"If the misery of the poor be caused not by the laws of nature, but by our institutions, great is our sin." Charles Darwin

"To a man with an empty stomach food is God." Gandhi

"For every talent that poverty has stimulated it has blighted a hundred." John Gardner

"The most terrible poverty is loneliness, and the feeling of being unloved." Mother Teresa

"But I, being poor, have only my dreams. I have spread my dreams under your feet; tread softly, because you tread on my dreams." William Butler Yeats

"Poverty often deprives a man of all spirit and virtue; it is hard for an empty bag to stand upright" Benjamin Franklin

"The inevitable consequence of poverty is dependence" Samuel Johnson

"There is something about poverty that smells like death." Zora Neale Hurston

"One must be poor to know the luxury of giving" George Eliot

"I thank fate for having made me born poor. Poverty taught me the true value of the gifts useful to life." Anatole France

Chapter 139 Power

"In order to obtain and hold power, a man must love it." Leo Tolstoy

"It is a mistake, that a lust for power is the mark of a great mind; for even the weakest have been captivated by it; and for minds of the highest order, it has no charms." Charles Caleb Colton

"Power gradually extirpates for the mind every humane and gentle virtue." Edmund Burke

"Wealth is power, and power is the only thing about which contemporary culture cares" Dean Koontz

"Absolute power was not meant for man." William E. Channing

"The best guarantee against the abuse of power consists in the freedom, the purity, and the frequency of popular elections." John Quincy Adams

"Justice and power must be brought together, so that whatever is just may be powerful, and whatever is powerful may be just." Blaise Pascal

"He is most powerful who has power over himself" Seneca

"I hope our wisdom will grow with our power, and teach us that the less we use our power the greater it will be." Thomas Jefferson

"Knowledge is power." Francis Bacon, Sr.

Chapter 140 Praise

"There are two things people want more than sex and money... recognition and praise." Mary Kay Ash

"The meanest, most contemptible kind of praise is that which first speaks well of a man, and then qualifies it with a But." Henry Ward Beecher

"Attach yourself to those who advise you rather than praise you." Nicholas Boileau

"A heap of epithets is poor praise: the praise lies in the facts, and in the way of telling them." Jean De La Bruyere

"What every genuine philosopher (every genuine man, in fact) craves most is praise -- although the philosophers generally call it recognition!" Henry James

"You do ill if you praise, but worse if you censure, what you do not understand." Leonardo da Vinci

"You can tell the character of every man when you see how he receives praise." Seneca

"Some criticism will be honest, some won't. Some praise you will deserve, some you won't. You can't let praise or criticism get to you. It's a weakness to get caught up in either one." John Wooden

"It would be a kind of ferocity to reject indifferently all sorts of praise. One should be glad to have that which comes from good men who praise in sincerity things that are really praiseworthy." Jean de La Bruyére

"Praise, like gold and diamonds, owes its value only to its scarcity."
Samuel Johnson

Chapter 141 Prayer

"If the only prayer you ever say in your entire life is thank you, it will be enough." Meister Eckhart

"Under certain circumstances, profanity provides a relief denied even to prayer." Mark Twain

"Prayer requires more of the heart than of the tongue." Adam Clarke

"A single grateful thought toward heaven is the most perfect prayer." Gotthold Ephraim Lessing

"Prayer should be the key of the day and the lock of the night." George Herbert

"Prayer is not asking. It is a longing of the soul. It is daily admission of one's weakness. It is better in prayer to have a heart without words than words without a heart." Mahatma Gandhi

"In prayer it is better to have a heart without words than words without a heart." Mahatma Gandhi

"Most people do not pray; they only beg." George Bernard Shaw

"A man does not serve God when he prays, for it is himself he is trying to serve" Thomas Paine

"Prayer is a wine which makes glad the heart of man" Bernard of Clairvaux

Chapter 142 Prejudice

"Everyone is a prisoner of his own experiences. No one can eliminate prejudices - just recognize them." Edward R. Murrow

"Criticism is prejudice made plausible." H. L. Mencken

"It is never too late to give up our prejudices." Henry David Thoreau

"Prejudices are what fools use for reason." Voltaire

"Many people think they are thinking when they are merely rearranging their prejudices." William James

"Travel is fatal to prejudice, bigotry, and narrow-mindedness." Mark Twain

"Great spirits have always found violent opposition from mediocrities. The latter cannot understand it when a man does not thoughtlessly submit to hereditary prejudices but honestly and courageously uses his intelligence." Albert Einstein

"Prejudice, not being founded on reason, cannot be removed by argument" Samuel Johnson

"Hypocrisy: prejudice with a halo" Ambrose Bierce

"The greatest friend of truth is Time, her greatest enemy is Prejudice, and her constant companion is Humility" Charles Caleb Colton

Chapter 143 Pride

"When dealing with people, let us remember we are not dealing with creatures of logic. We are dealing with creatures of emotion, creatures bustling with prejudices and motivated by pride and vanity." Dale Carnegie

"Generosity is giving more than you can, and pride is taking less than you need." Kahlil Gibran

"Proud people breed sad sorrows for themselves." Emily Bronte

"There is a paradox in pride--it makes some men ridiculous, but prevents others from becoming so." Charles Calob Colton

"Pride is a cold, stormy, barren mountain." John Thornton

"Pride, like cunning, is made offensive only by the manner in which it discovers itself." Norman MacDonald

"Pride is often the chief cause of our reproving others faults, that we may be thereby judged not guilty of the like errors." Wellins Calcotti

"The infinitely little have a pride infinitely great." Voltaire

"In general, pride is at the bottom of all great mistakes." John Ruskin

"Pride makes us artificial and humility makes us real." Thomas Merton

Chapter 144 Progress

"The chief obstacle to the progress of the human race is the human race." Don Marquis

"The reasonable man adapts himself to the world; the unreasonable one persists in trying to adapt the world to himself. Therefore all progress depends on the unreasonable man." George Bernard Shaw

"Usually, terrible things that are done with the excuse that progress requires them are not really progress at all, but just terrible things." Russell Baker

"The great thing in the world is not so much where we stand, as in what direction we are moving." Oliver Wendell Holmes

"Progress is man's ability to complicate simplicity." Thor-Heyerdahl

"Progress is made by lazy men looking for easier ways to do things" Robert A. Heinlein

"The test of our progress is not whether we add to the abundance of those who have much. It is whether we provide enough to those who have little." Franklin D. Roosevelt

"Progress imposes not only new possibilities for the future but new restrictions" Norbert Wiener

"All of us are guinea pigs in the laboratory of God. Humanity is just a work in progress." Tennessee Williams

"The first condition of progress is the removal of censorship." George Bernard Shaw

Chapter 145 Promises

"Promises are the uniquely human way of ordering the future, making it predictable and reliable to the extent that this is humanly possible." Hannah Arendt

"All promise outruns performance." Ralph Waldo Emerson

"He is poor indeed that can promise nothing." Thomas Fuller

"Promises are like crying babies in a theater, they should be carried out at once." Norman Vincent Peale

"An acre of performance is worth a whole world of promise." William Dean Howells

"Between today and tomorrow are graves, and between promising and fulfilling are chasms." Ruckett

"The person who is slowest in making a promise is most faithful in its performance." Jean Jacques Rousseau

"We must not promise what we ought not, lest we be called on to perform what we cannot." Abraham Lincoln

"For every promise, there is price to pay." Jim Rohn

"We promise according to our hopes and perform according to our fears." Francois De La Rochefoucauld

Chapter 146 Proverbs

"Examine what is said, not him who speaks." Arab Proverb

"Be not afraid of growing slowly, be afraid only of standing still."
Chinese Proverb

"He who asks is a fool for five minutes, but he who does not ask remains a fool forever." Chinese Proverb

"Wait until it is night before saying that it has been a fine day." French Proverb

"The reverse side also has a reverse side." Japanese Proverb

"Make sure to be in with your equals if you're going to fall out with your superiors." Jewish Proverb

"Don't think there are no crocodiles because the water is calm."
Malayan Proverb

"Go often to the house of thy friend; for weeds soon choke up the unused path." Scandinavian Proverb

"Whoever gossips to you will gossip about you." Spanish Proverb

"They who give have all things; they who withhold have nothing."
Indian Proverb

"If you live in the river you should make friends with the crocodile."
Indian proverb

Chapter 147 Questioning

"In all affairs it's a healthy thing now and then to hang a question mark on the things you have long taken for granted." Bertrand Russell

"Look at all the sentences which seem true and question them." David Reisman

"The most erroneous stories are those we think we know best - and therefore never scrutinize or question." Stephen Jay Gould

"Judge of a man by his questions rather than by his answers." Voltaire

"What we observe is not nature itself, but nature exposed to our method of questioning." Werner Heisenberg

"No simplicity of mind, no obscurity of station, can escape the universal duty of questioning all that we believe." William Kingdon Clifford

"I think of myself as being a relatively intelligent man who is open to a lot of different things and I think that questioning our purpose in life and the meaning of existence is something that we all go through at some point." Laurence Fishburne

"Who questions much, shall learn much, and retain much." Francis Bacon

"Millions saw the apple fall, but Newton was the one who asked why." Bernard Baruch

"Ask with urgency and passion." Arthur Balfour

Chapter 148 Quotations

"Quotation, n: The act of repeating erroneously the words of another." Ambrose Bierce

"Every book is a quotation; and every house is a quotation out of all forests, and mines, and stone quarries; and every man is a quotation from all his ancestors." Ralph Waldo Emerson

"A fine quotation is a diamond in the hand of a man of wit and a pebble in the hand of a fool." Joseph Roux

"The wisdom of the wise, and the experience of ages, may be preserved by quotation." Isaac D'Israeli

"An apt quotation is like a lamp which flings its light over the whole sentence." Letitia Elizabeth Landon

"I love quotations because it is a joy to find thoughts one might have, beautifully expressed with much authority by someone recognized wiser than oneself." Marlene Dietrich

"Quotations will tell the full measure of meaning, if you have enough of them." James Murray

"Life itself is a quotation." Jorge Luis Borges

"It is a pleasure to be able to quote lines to fit any occasion..." Abraham Lincoln

Chapter 149 Reality

"Reality is merely an illusion, albeit a very persistent one." Albert Einstein

"Reality is nothing but a collective hunch." Jane Wagner

"Reality is that which, when you stop believing in it, doesn't go away." Philip K. Dickt

"Humankind cannot stand very much reality." T. S. Eliot

"Reality leaves a lot to the imagination." John Lennon

"Literature adds to reality, it does not simply describe it. It enriches the necessary competencies that daily life requires and provides; and in this respect, it irrigates the deserts that our lives have already become." C.S. Lewis

"The human soul has still greater need of the ideal than of the real. It is by the real that we exist; it is by the ideal that we live." Victor Hugo

"Let us live for the beauty of our own reality." Charles Lamb

"Life is not a problem to be solved, but a reality to be experienced." Soren Kierkegaard

"The world of reality has its limits; the world of imagination is boundless." Jean-Jacques Rousseau

Chapter 150 Reason

"Reason is the slow and torturous method by which those who do not know the truth discover it." Blaise Pascal

"In my opinion, a life governed by reason is likely to be more dignified than one shaped by dogma and unbridled emotions." Nayef Al-Rodhan

"The intuitive mind is a sacred gift and the rational mind is a faithful servant. We have created a society that honors the servant and has forgotten the gift." Albert Einstein

"Intuition is reason in a hurry." Holbrook Jackson

"The most formidable weapon against errors of every kind is reason." Thomas Paine

"Reason is our soul's left hand, Faith her right." John Donne

"Reason is the natural order of truth; but imagination is the organ of meaning." C.S. Lewis

"Reason's last step is the recognition that there are an infinite number of things which are beyond it." Blaise Pascal

"As soon as we abandon our own reason, and are content to rely upon authority, there is no end to our troubles." Bertrand Russell

 "When I'm getting ready to reason with a man, I spend one-third of my time thinking about myself and what I am going to say -- and two-thirds thinking about him and what he is going to say." Abraham Lincoln

Chapter 151 Relaxation

"Man is so made that he can only find relaxation from one kind of labor by taking up another." Anatole France

"During [these] periods of relaxation after concentrated intellectual activity, the intuitive mind seems to take over and can produce the sudden clarifying insights which give so much joy and delight." Fritjof Capra

"The time to relax is when you don't have time for it." Sydney J. Harris

"The man who doesn't relax and hoot a few hoots voluntarily, now and then, is in great danger of hooting hoots and standing on his head for the edification of the pathologist and trained nurse, a little later on." Elbert Hubbard

"Taking time out each day to relax and renew is essential to living well." Judith Hanson Lasater

"Laughter relaxes. And relaxation is spiritual." Bhagwan Shree Rajneesh

"A cheerful frame of mind, reinforced by relaxation...is the medicine that puts all ghosts of fear on the run." George Matthew Adams

"No matter how much pressure you feel at work, if you could find ways to relax for at least five minutes every hour, you'd be more productive." Dr. Joyce Brothers

"Everything you do can be done better from a place of relaxation." Stephen C. Paul

"Every now and then go away, have a little relaxation, for when you come back to your work your judgment will be surer. Go some distance away because then the work appears smaller and more of it can be taken in at a glance and a lack of harmony and proportion is more readily seen." Leonardo da Vinci

Chapter 152 Religion

"My religion consists of a humble admiration of the illimitable superior spirit who reveals himself in the slight details we are able to perceive with our frail and feeble mind." Albert Einstein

"Everyone ought to worship God according to his own inclinations, and not to be constrained by force." Flavius Josephus

"Say nothing of my religion. It is known to God and myself alone. Its evidence before the world is to be sought in my life: if it has been honest and dutiful to society the religion which has regulated it cannot be a bad one." Thomas Jefferson

"We have just enough religion to make us hate, but not enough to make us love one another." Jonathan Swift

"When we blindly adopt a religion, a political system, a literary dogma, we become automatons. We cease to grow." Anais Nin

"What difference does it make how much you have? What you do not have amounts to much more." Seneca

"Many have quarreled about religion that never practiced it" Benjamin Franklin

"I believe that the very purpose of our life is to seek happiness. That is clear. Whether one believes in religion or not, whether one believes in this religion or that religion, we all are seeking something better in life. So, I think, the very motion of our life is towards happiness..." Dalai Lama

"Buddhism has the characteristics of what would be expected in a cosmic religion for the future: It transcends a personal God, avoids dogmas and theology; it covers both the natural and spritual; and it is based on a religious sense aspiring from the experience of all things, natural and spiritual, as a meaningful unity." Albert Einstein

"Religion is the manifestation of the Divinity already in man" Swami Vivekananda

Chapter 153 Reputation

"You can't build a reputation on what you are going to do." Henry Ford

"My reputation grows with every failure." George Bernard Shaw

"It takes many good deeds to build a good reputation, and only one bad one to lose it" Benjamin Franklin

"It takes 20 years to build a reputation and five minutes to ruin it. If you think about that, you'll do things differently." Warren Buffett

"The solar system has no anxiety about its reputation" Ralph Waldo Emerson

"A reputation once broken may possibly be repaired, but the world will always keep their eyes on the spot where the crack was." Joseph Hall

"Never make negative comments or spread rumors about anyone. It depreciates their reputation and yours." Brian Koslow

"Reputation is only a candle, of wavering and uncertain flame, and easily blown out, but it is the light by which the world looks for and finds merit." James Russell Lowell

"It pays to be obvious, especially if you have a reputation for subtlety." Isaac Asimov

"There is no advertisement as powerful as a positive reputation traveling fast." Brian Koslow

Chapter 154 Respect

"The way to procure insults is to submit to them: a man meets with no more respect than he exacts." William Hazlitt

"Men are respectable only as they respect" Ralph Waldo Emerson

"I'm not concerned with your liking or disliking me... All I ask is that you respect me as a human being." Jackie Robinson

"When you are content to be simply yourself and don't compare or compete, everybody will respect you." Lao-Tzu

"There was no respect for youth when I was young, and now that I am old, there is no respect for age--I missed it coming and going." J. B. Priestly

"Being brilliant is no great feat if you respect nothing." Johann Wolfgang von Goethe

"To be sensual, I think, is to respect and rejoice in the force of life, of life itself, and to be present in all that one does, from the effort of loving to the making of bread." James Arthur Baldwin

"Nothing is more despicable than respect based on fear." Albert Camus

"Show respect to all people, but grovel to none." Tecumseh

"If we desire respect for the law, we must first make the law respectable." Louis D. Brandeis.

Chapter 155 Responsibility

"We are made wise not by the recollection of our past, but by the responsibility for our future." George Bernard Shaw

"Action springs not from thought, but from a readiness for responsibility." Dietrich Bonhoeffer

"No man was ever endowed with a right without being at the same time saddled with a responsibility." Gerald W. Johnson

"It is the responsibility of leadership to provide opportunity, and the responsibility of individuals to contribute." William Pollard

"The first responsibility of a leader is to define reality. The last is to say thank you. In between, the leader is a servant." Max De Pree

"In times like these men should utter nothing for which they would not be willingly responsible through time and in eternity." Abraham Lincoln

"Our greatest responsibility is to be good ancestors" Jonas Salk

"Nothing strengthens the judgment and quickens the conscience like individual responsibility." Elizabeth Cady Stanton

"The disappearance of a sense of responsibility is the most far-reaching consequence of submission to authority." Stanley Milgram

"Sin with the multitude, and your responsibility and guilt are as great and as truly personal, as if you alone had done the wrong" Tryon Edwards

Chapter 156 Revenge

"I tasted too what was called the sweet of revenge - but it was transient, it expired even with the object, that provoked it." Ann Radcliffe

"An eye for an eye makes the whole world blind." Mahatma Gandhi

"In taking revenge, a man is but even with his enemy; but in passing it over, he is superior." Sir Francis Bacon

"Revenge is always the weak pleasure of a little and narrow mind" Juvenal

"Revenge is an act of passion; vengeance of justice. Injuries are revenged; crimes are avenged." Samuel Johnson

"Revenge... is like a rolling stone, which, when a man hath forced up a hill, will return upon him with a greater violence, and break those bones whose sinews gave it motion." Albert Schweitzer

"Justice belongs to those who claim it, but let the claimant beware lest he create new injustice by his claim and thus set the bloody pendulum of revenge into its inexorable motion" Frank Herbert

"Revenge has no more quenching effect on emotions than salt water has on thirst." Walter Weckler

"Revenge proves its own executioner." John Ford

"The best revenge is to be unlike him who performed the injury." Marcus Aurelius

Chapter 157 Revolution

"The time to stop a revolution is at the beginning, not the end." Adlai Stevenson

"In a revolution, as in a novel. the most difficult part to invent is the end." Alexis de Tocqueville

"Those who make peaceful revolution impossible will make violent revolution inevitable." John F. Kennedy

"Every revolution evaporates and leaves behind only the slime of a new bureaucracy." Franz Kafka

"Revolution is the festival of the oppressed." Germaine Greer

"We decry violence all the time in this country, but look at our history. We were born in a violent revolution, and we've been in wars ever since. We're not a pacific people." James Lee Burke

"In the last five or six thousand years, empires one after another have arisen, waxed powerful by wars of conquest, and fallen by internal revolution or attack from without." John Boyd Orr

"We have confirmed something we only knew in theory, namely that revolution, in which uncontrolled and uncontrollable forces operate imperiously, is blind and destructive, grandiose and cruel." Frederica Montseny

"Every successful revolution puts on in time the robes of the tyrant it has deposed." Barbara Tuchman

"We need an energy revolution by breaking our dependence on fossil fuels, polluting fuels... I am very, very confident our small state will lead this. We will be noticed by the country and the world." Bernie Sanders

Chapter 158 Risk

"If you don't risk anything you risk even more." Erica Jong

"Take calculated risks. That is quite different from being rash." George S. Patton

"Our lives improve only when we take chances - and the first and most difficult risk we can take is to be honest with ourselves." Walter Anderson

"Progress always involves risks. You can't steal second base and keep your foot on first." Frederick B. Wilcox

"Yes, risk taking is inherently failure-prone. Otherwise, it would be called sure-thing-taking." Tim McMahon

"The person who risks nothing, does nothing, has nothing, is nothing, and becomes nothing. He may avoid suffering and sorrow, but he simply cannot learn and feel and change and grow and love and live." Leo F. Buscaglia

"Often the difference between a successful person and a failure is not one has better abilities or ideas, but the courage that one has to bet on one's ideas, to take a calculated risk - and to act." Andre Malraux

"He who risks and fails can be forgiven. He who never risks and never fails is a failure in his whole being." Paul Tillich

"It is only by risking our persons from one hour to another that we live at all." William James

"No noble thing can be done without risks" Michel de Montaigne

Chapter 159 Rules

"You have to learn the rules of the game. And then you have to play better than anyone else." Albert Einstein

"Hell, there are no rules here - we're trying to accomplish something." Thomas A. Edison

"The golden rule is that there are no golden rules." George Bernard Shaw

"Integrity has no need of rules." Albert Camus

"For generations, Americans who aren't rich have been generous and admiring of their wealthy compatriots - want a country where people who work hard can succeed, where the same rules apply to everyone. They expect to have their own shot at getting rich. But increasingly, they are seeing that the game is rigged." Dee Dee Myers

"The only rules comedy can tolerate are those of taste, and the only limitations those of libel."James Thurber

"I believe in rules. Sure I do. If there weren't any rules, how could you break them?" Leo Durocher

"Chess helps you to concentrate, improve your logic. It teaches you to play by the rules and take responsibility for your actions, how to problem solve in an uncertain environment." Garry Kasparov

"If you are a genius, you'll make your own rules, but if not - and the odds are against it - go to your desk no matter what your mood, face the icy challenge of the paper - write." J. B. Priestley

"Consulting the rules of composition before taking a photograph, is like consulting the laws of gravity before going for a walk." Edward Weston

Chapter 160 Sanity

"In a mad world only the mad are sane." Akira Kurosawa

"Part of being sane, is being a little bit crazy." Janet Long

"Sanity calms, but madness is more interesting." John Russell

"Sanity is a cozy lie." Susan Sontag

"Sanity and happiness are an impossible combination" Mark Twain

"No man is sane who does not know how to be insane on the proper occasions." Henry Ward Beecher

"Sanity - that which is within the frame of reference of conventional thought" Erich Fromm

"One of the definitions of sanity is the ability to tell real from unreal. Soon we'll need a new definition." Alvin Toffler

"Facts by themselves can often feed the flame of madness, because sanity is a spirit." G.K. Chesterton

"Sanity means the wholeness of the consciousness. And our society is only part conscious, like an idiot." D.H Lawrence

"Sanity becomes the fantasy that keeps us sane; a rhetorical prop in an unplotted, threatening world." Adam Phillips

Chapter 161 Science

"Science has proof without any certainty. Creationists have certainty without any proof." Ashley Montague

"Science may set limits to knowledge, but should not set limits to imagination." Bertrand Russell

"There are in fact two things, science and opinion; the former begets knowledge, the latter ignorance." Hippocrates

"That is the essence of science: ask an impertinent question, and you are on your way to the pertinent answer." Jacob Bronowski

"I am among those who think that science has great beauty. A scientist in his laboratory is not only a technician: he is also a child placed before natural phenomena which impress him like a fairy tale." Marie Curie

"There is something fascinating about science. One gets such wholesale returns of conjecture out of such a trifling investment of fact." Mark Twain

"A new scientific truth does not triumph by convincing its opponents and making them see the light, but rather because its opponents eventually die, and a new generation grows up that is familiar with it." Max Planck

"It would be possible to describe everything scientifically, but it would make no sense; it would be without meaning, as if you described a Beethoven symphony as a variation of wave pressure." Albert Einstein

"Science progresses best when observations force us to alter our preconceptions" Vera Rubin

"Science and art belong to the whole world, and before them vanish the barriers of nationality" Johann Wolfgang von Goethe

"When Kepler found his long-cherished belief did not agree with the most precise observation, he accepted the uncomfortable fact. He preferred the hard truth to his dearest illusions; that is the heart of science." Carl Sagan

Chapter 162 Secrets

"Everything secret degenerates, even the administration of justice; nothing is safe that does not show how it can bear discussion and publicity." Lord Acton

"Secrecy is the badge of fraud." Sir John Chadwick

"I know that's a secret, for it's whispered everywhere." William Congreve

"Your secret is your prisoner; once you reveal it, you become its slave." Solomon Ibn Gabirol

"How can we accept another to keep our secret if we have been unable to keep it ourselves." Francois De La Rochefoucauld

"Three may keep a secret, if two of them are dead." Benjamin Franklin

"Secrets are made to be found out with time." Charles Sanford

"The man who can keep a secret may be wise, but he is not half as wise as the man with no secrets to keep" Edgar Watson Howe

"The wise have a solid sense of silence and the ability to keep a storehouse of secrets. Their capacity and character are respected." Baltasar Gracian

"None are so fond of secrets as those who do not mean to keep them." Charles Caleb Colton

"Confession is always weakness. The grave soul keeps its own secrets, and takes its own punishment in silence." Dorothy Dix

Chapter 163 Security

"There is no security on this earth, there is only opportunity." General Douglas MacArthur

"Too many people are thinking of security instead of opportunity. They seem more afraid of life than death." James F. Byrnes

"Uncertainty is the only certainty there is, and knowing how to live with insecurity is the only security." John Allen Paulos

"Security is when everything is settled. When nothing can happen to you. Security is the denial of life." Germaine Greer

"He who is firmly seated in authority soon learns to think security, and not progress, the highest lesson of statecraft. James Russell Lowell

"Security is the mother of danger and the grandmother of destruction." Thomas Fuller

"The more you seek security, the less of it you have. But the more you seek opportunity, the more likely it is that you will achieve the security that you desire." Brian Tracy

"In todays world, the security of every one of us is linked to that of everyone else." Kofi Atta Annan

"The search for static security-in the law and elsewhere-is misguided. The fact is . . . security can only be achieved through constant change, through discarding old ideas that have outlived their usefulness and adapting to current facts." William Orville Douglas

Chapter 164 Selfishness

"Those who do not hate their own selfishness and regard themselves as more important than the rest of the world are blind because the truth lies elsewhere" Blaise Pascal

"Selfishness is that detestable vice which no one will forgive in others, and no one is without in himself" Henry Ward Beecher

"Selfishness is the greatest curse of the human race" William E. Gladstone

"Modesty and unselfishness: These are the virtues which men praise, and pass by" Andre Maurois

"All sympathy not consistent with acknowledged virtue is but disguised selfishness" Samuel Taylor Coleridge

"Just as a fire is covered by smoke and a mirror is obscured by dust, just as the embryo rests deep within the womb, wisdom is hidden by selfish desire." Bhagavad Gita

"Human history is the sad result of each one looking out for himself." Julio Cortazar

"Manifest plainness, Embrace simplicity, Reduce selfishness, Have few desires." Lao Tzu

"If all the people in this world, in which we live, were as selfish as a few of the people in this world, in which we live, there would be no world in which to live." W. L. Orme

"Take the selfishness out of this world and there would be more happiness than we should know what to do with." Henry Wheeler

Chapter 165 Service

"It is high time that the ideal of success should be replaced by the ideal of service" Albert Einstein

"Teach this triple truth to all: A generous heart, kind speech, and a life of service and compassion are the things which renew humanity." Buddha

"The best way to find yourself is to lose yourself in the service of others." Mahatma Gandhi

"Start where you are. Distant fields always look greener, but opportunity lies right where you are. Take advantage of every opportunity of service." Robert Collier

"Greatness is not found in possessions, power, position, or prestige. It is discovered in goodness, humility, service, and character." William Arthur Ward

"How can I be useful, of what service can I be? There is something inside me, what can it be?" Vincent van Gogh

"A business absolutely devoted to service will have only one worry about profits. They will be embarrassingly large." Henry Ford

"Service to others is the rent you pay for your room here on earth." Shirley Chisholm

"All men seek one goal : success or happiness. The only way to achieve true success is to express yourself completely in service to society. First, have a definite, clear, practical ideal-a goal, an objective. Second, have the necessary means to achieve it." Aristotle

"Every day use your magic to be of service to others." Marcia Wieder

Chapter 166 Sex

"In America sex is an obsession, in other parts of the world it is a fact." Marlene Dietrich

"Anybody who believes that the way to a man's heart is through his stomach flunked geography." Robert Byrne

"Don't knock masturbation - it's sex with someone I love." Woody Allen

"Sex relieves tension - love causes it." Woody Allen

"Sex without love is an empty experience, but as empty experiences go it's one of the best." Woody Allen

"Men reach their sexual peak at eighteen. Women reach theirs at thirty-five. Do you get the feeling that God is playing a practical joke?" Rita Rudner

"My wife is a sex object. Every time I ask for sex, she objects." Les Dawson

"Civilized people cannot fully satisfy their sexual instinct without love." Bertrand Russell

"Boys and girls in America have such a sad time together; sophistication demands that they submit to sex immediately without proper preliminary talk. Not courting talk -- real straight talk about souls, for life is holy and every moment is precious." Jack Kerouac

"I think it is funny that we were freer about sexuality in the 4th century B.C. It is a little disconcerting." Angelina Jolie

Chapter 167 Silence

"He who does not know how to be silent will not know how to speak." Ausonius

"Silence is the most perfect expression of scorn." George Bernard Shaw

"A good word is an easy obligation; but not to speak ill, requires only our silence, which costs nothing." John Tillotson

"I have often regretted my speech, never my silence." Publilius Syrus

"It is better wither to be silent, or to say things of more value than silence. Sooner throw a pearl at hazard than an idle or useless word; and do not say a little in many words, but a great deal in a few." Pythagoras

"It is a great thing to know the season for speech and the season for silence." Seneca

"Silence is a source of great strength." Lao Tzu

"Music and silence combine strongly because music is done with silence, and silence is full of music." Marcel Marceau

"Silence is the true friend that never betrays." Confucius

"Let us be silent, that we may hear the whispers of the gods." Ralph Waldo Emerson

Chapter 168 Simplicity

**"Everything should be made as simple as possible, but not simpler."
Albert Einstein**

"Simplicity is the ultimate sophistication." Leonardo da Vinci

"A vocabulary of truth and simplicity will be of service throughout your life" Winston Churchill

"In character, in manner, in style, in all things, the supreme excellence is simplicity." Henry Wadsworth Longfellow

"Simplicity is the final achievement. After one has played a vast quantity of notes and more notes, it is simplicity that emerges as the crowning reward of art." Frederic Chopin

"The aspects of things that are most important for us are hidden because of their simplicity and familiarity" Ludwig Wittgensteinl

"Nothing is true, but that which is simple." Johann Wolfgang von Goethe

"I would not give a fig for the simplicity this side of complexity, but I would give my life for the simplicity on the other side of complexity."
Oliver Wendell Holmes

"Simplicity is making the journey of this life with just baggage enough."
Charles Dudley Warner

"The great seal of truth is simplicity." Herman Boerhaave

Chapter 169 Sincerity

**"Insincerity is always weakness; sincerity even in error is strength."
George Henry Lewes**

"Sincerity is impossible, unless it pervade the whole being, and the pretence of it saps the very foundation of character." James Russell Lowell

"Sincerity is an openness of heart; we find it in very few people; what we usually see is only an artful dissimulation to win the confidence of others." Francois De La Rochefoucauld

"Sincerity makes the very least person to be of more value than the most talented hypocrite." Charles Spurgeon

"As you put into practice the qualities of patience, punctuality, sincerity, and solicitude, you will have a better opinion of the world around you" Grenville Kleiser

"Being brilliant is no great feat if you respect nothing." Johann Wolfgang von Goethe

"No man can produce great things who is not thoroughly sincere in dealing with himself" James Russell

"I sat at a table where were rich food and wine in abundance, and obsequious attendance, but sincerity and truth were not; and I went away hungry from the inhospitable board." Henry David Thoreau

"Those that vow the most are the least sincere." Richard Brinsley Sheridan

"Sincerity and competence is a strong combination. In politics, it is everything." Peggy Noonan

Chapter 170 Sleep

**"Sleeping is no mean art: for its sake one must stay awake all day."
Friedrich Nietzsche**

"It is a common experience that a problem difficult at night is resolved in the morning after the committee of sleep has worked on it." John Steinbeck

"The amount of sleep required by the average person is five minutes more." Wilson Mizener

"Sleep is the best meditation." Dalai Lama

"The best cure for insomnia is to get a lot of sleep." W. C. Fields

"Man should forget his anger before he lies down to sleep." Mahatma Gandhi

"That we are not much sicker and much madder than we are is due exclusively to that most blessed and blessing of all natural graces, sleep." Aldous Huxley

"Some people talk in their sleep. Lecturers talk while other people sleep." Albert Camus

"When action grows unprofitable, gather information; when information grows unprofitable, sleep." Ursula K. Le Guin

"No man should ever lose sleep over public affairs." Harold MacMillan

Chapter 171 Snow

"Lo. sifted through the winds that blow, Down comes the soft and silent snow, White petals from the flowers that grow In the cold atmosphere." George W. Bungay

"Sunshine is delicious, rain is refreshing, wind braces us up, snow is exhilarating; there is really no such thing as bad weather, only different kinds of good weather." John Ruskin

"When I no longer thrill to the first snow of the season, I'll know I'm growing old." Lady Bird Johnson

"I love snow, snow, and all the forms of radiant frost." Percy Bysshe Shelley

"Resting on your laurels is as dangerous as resting when you are walking in the snow. You doze off and die in your sleep." Ludwig Wittgenstein

"The snow itself is lonely or, if you prefer, self-sufficient. There is no other time when the whole world seems composed of one thing and one thing only." Joseph Wood Krutch

"There is nothing in the world more beautiful than the forest clothed to its very hollows in snow. It is the still ecstasy of nature, wherein every spray, every blade of grass, every spire of reed, every intricacy of twig, is clad with radiance." William Sharp

"Until I came to Canada I never knew 'snow' was a four letter word" Alberto Manguel

"There is still vitality under the winter snow, even though to the casual eye it seems to be dead" Agnes Sligh Turnbull

"Advice is like snow - the softer it falls, the longer it dwells upon, and the deeper in sinks into the mind." Samuel Taylor Coleridge

"Even in winter an isolated patch of snow has a special quality." Andy Goldsworthy

Chapter 172 Society

"The nature of society is largely determined by the direction in which talent and ambition flow-by the tilt of the social landscape." Eric Hoffer

"I'm against a homogenized society, because I want the cream to rise." Robert Frost

"There is no nonsense so gross that society will not, at some time, make a doctrine of it and defend it with every weapon of communal stupidity." Robertson Davies

"I think we risk becoming the best informed society that has ever died of ignorance." Reuben Blades

"Nothing can be more readily disproved than the old saw, "You can't keep a good man down." Most human societies have been beautifully organized to keep good men down." John W. Gardner

"How can a society that exists on instant mashed potatoes, packaged cake mixes, frozen dinners, and instant cameras teach patience to its young?" Paul Sweeney

"Society honors its living conformists and its dead troublemakers." Mignon McLaughlin

"Society knows perfectly well how to kill a man and has methods more subtle than death" Andre Gide

"Society is a masked ball, where every one hides his real character, and reveals it by hiding" Ralph Waldo Emerson

"A civilized society is one which tolerates eccentricity to the point of doubtful sanity." Robert Frost

Chapter 173 Speech

"Free speech carries with it some freedom to listen." Bob Marley

"The superior man is modest in his speech, but exceeds in his actions." Confucius

"What this country needs is more free speech worth listening to." Hansell B. Duckett

"Today's public figures can no longer write their own speeches or books, and there is some evidence that they can't read them either." Gore Vidal

"Do not fight verbosity with words: speech is given to all, intelligence to few." Moralia

"Speech is human, silence is divine, yet also brutish and dead: therefore we must learn both arts." Thomas Carlyle

"If nobody spoke unless he had something to say, the human race would very soon lose the use of speech." W. Somerset Maugham

"Why doesn't the fellow who says, "I'm no speechmaker," let it go at that instead of giving a demonstration?" Kin Hubbard

"Public speaking is the art of diluting a two-minute idea with a two-hour vocabulary." Evan Esar

"Speech is power: speech is to persuade, to convert, to compel. It is to bring another out of his bad sense into your good sense." Ralph Waldo Emerson

Chapter 174 Sports

"Sports do not build character. They reveal it." John Wooden

"Sports is the toy department of human life." Howard Cosell

"Sport is the habitual and voluntary cultivation of intensive physical effort." Pierre de Coubertin

"Football incorporates the two worst elements of American society: violence punctuated by committee meetings." George F. Will

"The mark of great sportsmen is not how good they are at their best, but how good they are their worst." Martina Navratilova

"Do you know what my favorite part of the game is? The opportunity to play." Mike Singletary

"I believe in rules. Sure I do. If there weren't any rules, how could you break them?" Leo Durocher

"Chess helps you to concentrate, improve your logic. It teaches you to play by the rules and take responsibility for your actions, how to problem solve in an uncertain environment." Garry Kasparov

 "A good hockey player plays where the puck is. A great hockey player plays where the puck is going to be." Wayne Gretzky

"Sports are a microcosm of society"Billie Jean King

"Winning isn't everything, but playing and competing and striving and going through things can be a lot of fun and really important. As long as you're doing it in a way that's healthy, sports can be an incredible opportunity"Andrew Shue

Chapter 175 Spring

"In the spring, at the end of the day, you should smell like dirt."
Margaret Atwood.

"An optimist is the human personification of spring." Susan J. Bissonette

"Spring shows what God can do with a drab and dirty world." Virgil A. Kraft

"Spring has returned. The earth is like a child that knows poems." Rainer Maria Rilke

"Sanity and happiness are an impossible combination" Mark Twain

"Spring: An experience in immortality." Henry David Thoreau

"Spring makes its own statement, so loud and clear that the gardener seems to be only one of the instruments, not the composer" Geoffrey B. Charlesworth

"If I had to life to live over, I would start barefoot earlier in the spring and stay that way later in the fall." Nadine Stair "Spring being a tough act to follow, God created June." Al Bernstein

"A hush is over everything, Silent as women wait for love; The world is waiting for the spring." Sara Teasdale

"Winter is etching, spring a watercolor, summer an oil painting and autumn a mosaic of them all" Stanley Horowitz

Chapter 176 Statistics

"Statistical thinking will one day be as necessary a qualification for efficient citizenship as the ability to read and write." H.G. Wells

"Do not put faith in what statistics say until you have carefully considered what they do not say." William W. Watt

"Statistics are like a bikini. What they reveal is suggestive, but what they conceal is vital." Aaron Levenstein

"The invalid assumption that correlation implies cause is probably the two or three most serious and common errors of human reasoning." Stephen Jay Gould

"He uses statistics as a drunken man uses lamp-posts- for support rather than illumination." Andrew Lang

"Statistics: The only science that enables different experts using the same figures to draw different conclusions." Evan Esar

"There are three kinds of lies: lies, damned lies, and statistics." Benjamin Disraeli

"Torture numbers, and they will confess to anything." Gregg Easterbrook

"Statistician: A man who believes figures don't lie, but admits under analysis that some of them won't stand up either." Evan Esar

"It is the mark of a truly intelligent person to be moved by statistics." George Bernard Shaw

Chapter 177 Stress

"Stress should be a powerful driving force, not an obstacle." Bill Phillips

"The man who doesn't relax and hoot a few hoots voluntarily, now and then, is in great danger of hooting hoots and standing on his head for the edification of the pathologist and trained nurse, a little later on." Elbert Hubbard

"Stress is nothing more than a socially acceptable form of mental illness." Richard Carlson

"Give your stress wings and let it fly away." Terri Guilllemets

"Stress is an ignorant state. It believes that everything is an emergency." Natalie Goldberg

"Stress is the trash of modern life – we all generate it but if you don't dispose of it properly, it will pile up and overtake your life." Terri Guillemets

"Stress is poison." Agave powers

"In times of great stress or adversity, it's always best to keep busy, to plow your anger and your energy into something positive." Lee Iacocca

"Reality is the leading cause of stress for those in touch with it." Jack Wagner

"Stress is an important dragon to slay- or at least tame- in your life." Marilu Henner

Chapter 178 Stupidity

"The difference between genius and stupidity is that genius has its limits." Albert Einstein

"Nothing in the world is more dangerous than sincere ignorance and conscientious stupidity." Martin Luther King, Jr.

"Against stupidity the very gods themselves contend in vain." Friedrich Schiller

"Stupidity is an elemental force for which no earthquake is a match." Karl Kraus

"Creativity is the sudden cessation of stupidity." Edwin Land

"Stupidity is the deliberate cultivation of ignorance." William Gaddis

"Stupidity combined with arrogance and a huge ego will get you a long way." Chris Lowe

"Stupidity trumps Machiavelli almost every time when you are looking for an explanation." Robert Foster Bennett

"The two most common elements in the universe are hydrogen and stupidity." Harlan Ellison

"Whenever a man does a thoroughly stupid thing, it is always from the noblest motives." Oscar Wilde

Chapter 179 Success

"If A is success in life, the A equals x plus y plus z. Work is x; y is play; and z is keeping your mouth shut." Albert Einstein

"Try not be a man of success but rather to become a man of value." Albert Einstein

"There is only one success... to be able to spend your life in your own way, and not to give others absurd maddening claims upon it." Christopher Morley

"Success consists of going from failure to failure without loss of enthusiasm." Winston Churchill

"I dread success. To have succeeded is to have finished one's business on earth, like a male spider, who is killed by the female the moment he has succeeded in courtship. I like a state of continual becoming, with a goal in front and not behind." George Bernard Shaw

"That man is successful who has lived well, laughed often, and loved much, who has gained the respect of the intelligent men and the love of children; who has filled his niche and accomplished his task; who leaves the world better than he found it, whether by an improved poppy, a perfect poem, or a rescued soul; who never lacked the appreciation of earth's beauty or failed to express it; who looked for the best in others and gave the best he had." Robert Louis Stephenson

"Success is more permanent when you achieve it without destroying your principles." Walter Kronkite

"Success seems to be largely a matter of hanging on after others have let go." William Feather

"Success is 99 percent failure." Soichiro Honda

"Success and failure. We think of them as opposites, but they're really not. They're companions- the hero and the sidekick." Laurence Shames

Chapter 180 Suffering

**"Although the world is full of suffering, it is also full of overcoming it."
Helen Keller**

"Wisdom comes alone through suffering." Aeschylus

"Suffering is part of the divine idea." Henry Ward Beecher

"For suffering and enduring, there is no remedy but striving and doing."
Thomas Carlyle

"It is the lot of man to suffer." Benjamin Disraeli

"Out of suffering have emerged the strongest souls; the most massive
characters are seared with scars." Kahlil Gibran

"If you suffer, thank God! – it is a sure sign that you are alive." Elbert
Hubbard

"Suffering, once accepted, loses its edge, for the terror of it lessens,
and what remains is generally far more manageable than we had
imagined." Lesley Hazelton

"Suffering is the price of being alive and it is music and singing and art
that has helped me live through some of the most difficult things that
have happened to me." Judy Collins

"Suffering is but another name for the teaching of experience, which is
the parent of instruction and the schoolmaster of life." Horace

Greatness is not found in possessions, power, position, or prestige. It is
discovered in goodness, humility, service, and character." William
Arthur Ward

"How can I be useful, of what service can I be? There is something inside me, what can it be?" Vincent van Gogh

"A business absolutely devoted to service will have only one worry about profits. They will be embarrassingly large." Henry Ford

"Service to others is the rent you pay for your room here on earth." Shirley Chisholm

"All men seek one goal : success or happiness. The only way to achieve true success is to express yourself completely in service to society. First, have a definite, clear, practical ideal-a goal, an objective. Second, have the necessary means to achieve it." Aristotle

 "Every day use your magic to be of service to others." Marcia Wieder

Chapter 181 Summer

"Summer is a promissory note signed in June, its long days spent and gone before you know it, and due to be repaid next January." Hal Borland

"In the depth of winter, I finally learned that within me there lay an invincible summer." Albert Camus

"Summer afternoon – Summer afternoon... the two most beautiful words in the English language." Henry James

"Deep summer is when laziness finds respectability." Sam Keen

"The summer night is like a perfection of thought." Wallace Stevens

"In summer, the song sings itself." William Carlos Williams

"Ah, summer, what power you have to make us suffer and like it." Russel Baker

"A perfect summer day is when the sun is shining, the breeze is blowing, the birds are singing, and the lawn mower is broken." James Dent

"Spring passes and one remembers one's innocence. Summer passes and one remembers one's exuberance. Autumn passes and one remembers one's reverence. Winter passes and one remembers ones perseverance." Yoko Ono

"There shall be eternal summer in the grateful heart." Celia Thaxter

Chapter 182 Superstition

"Superstition is to religion what astrology is to astronomy: the mad daughter of a wise mother." Voltaire

"Fear is the main source of superstition, and one of the main sources of cruelty. To conquer fear is the beginning of wisdom." Bertrand Rusell

"Men become superstitious, not because they have too much imagination, but because they are not aware they have any." George Santayana

"Superstition is the spleen of the soul." Alexander Pope

"The root of all superstition is that men observe when a thing hits, but not when it misses." Francis Bacon

"Superstition brings the gods into even the smallest matters." Titus Livy

"Superstition is the only religion of which base souls are capable." Joseph Joubert

"The only foes that threaten America are the enemies at home, and these are ignorance, superstition and incompetence." Elbert Hubbard

"A belief which leaves no place for doubt is not a belief; it is a superstition." Jose Bergamin

Chapter 183 Talent

"Hide not your talents, they for use were made. What's a sun-dial in the shade?" Benjamin Franklin

"Everyone has talent. What is rare is the courage to follow talent to te dark place where it leads." Erica Jong

"Getting ahead in a difficult profession requires avid faith in yourself. That why some people with mediocre talent, but great inner drive, go much further than people with vastly superior talent." Sophia Loren

"I have no particular talent. I am merely inquisitive." Albert Einstein

"A really great talent finds its happiness in execution." Johann Wolfgang von Goethe

"Talent without discipline is like an octopus on roller skates. There's plenty of movement, but you never know if it's going to be forward, backwards, or sideways." H. Jackson Brown, Jr.

"The most exciting place to discover talent is in yourself." Ashleigh Brilliant

"I believe that every person is born with talent." Maya Angelou

"Talent is God given. Be humble. Fame is man-given. Be grateful. Conceit is self-given. Be careful." John Wooden

"The most valuable of all talents is never using two words when one will do." Thomas Jefferson

Chapter 184 Taxes

"The nation should have a tax system that looks like someone designed it on purpose." William Sinon

"Capital punishment: The income tax." Jeff Hayes

"Man is not like other animals in the ways that are really significant: animals have instincts, we have taxes." Erving Goffman

"Philosophy teach a man that he can't take it with him; taxes teach him he can't leave it behind either." Mignon McLaughlin

"We are told that this is an odious and unpopular tax. I never knew a tax that was not odious and unpopular with the people who paid it." John Sherman

"If we don't do something to simplify the tax system, we're going to end up with a national police force of internal revenue agents." Leon Panetta

"Tax complexity itself is a kind of tax." Joseph Bonkowski

"Taxes are what we pay for a civilized society" Oliver Wendell Holmes

 "The American colonies, all know, were greatly opposed to taxation without representation. They were also, a less celebrated quality, equally opposed to taxation with representation." John Kenneth Galbraith

Chapter 185 Teaching

"The dream begins with a teacher who believes in you, who tugs and pushes and leads you to the next plateau, sometimes poking you with a sharp stick called "truth"." Dan Rather

"In teaching you cannot see the fruit of a day's work. It is invisible and remains so, maybe for twenty years." Jacques Barzun

"If a doctor, lawyer, or dentist had 40 people in his office at a time, all of whom had different needs, and some of whom didn't want to be there and was causing trouble, and the doctor, lawyer, or dentist, without assistance, had to treat them all with professional excellence for nine months, then he might have some conception of the classroom teacher's job." Donald D. Quinn

"Modern cynics and skeptics,, see no harm in paying those to whom they entrust the minds of their children a smaller wage than is paid to whom they entrust the care of their plumbing." John F. Kennedy

"A teacher is one who makes himself progressively unnecessary." Thomas Carruthers

"A teacher affects eternity; he can never tell where his influence stops." Henry Brooks Adams

"A good teacher is a master of simplification and an enemy of simplism." Louis A. Berman

"The best teacher is the one who suggests rather than dogmatizes, and inspires his listener with the wish to teach himself." Edward Bulwer-Lytton

"Teaching is not a lost art, but the regard for it is a lost tradition." Jacques Barzun

"One looks back with appreciation to the brilliant teachers, but with gratitude to those who touched our human feelings. The curriculum is so much necessary raw material, but warmth is the vital element for the growing plant and for the soul of the child." Carl Jung

Chapter 186 Technology

**"Technology is just a tool. In terms of getting the kids working together and motivating them, the teacher is the most important."
Bill Gates**

"Technological progress has merely provided us with more efficient means for going backwards." Aldous Huxley

"If it keeps up, man will atrophy all his limbs but the push-button finger." Frank Lloyd Wright

"Technology is the knack of so arranging the world we don't have to experience it." Max Frisch

"All of the biggest technological inventions created by man- the airplane, the automobile, the computer – says little about his intelligence, but speaks volumes about his laziness" Mark Kennedy

"It has become appallingly obvious that our technology has exceeded our humanity." Albert Einstein

"For a successful technology, reality must take precedence over public relations, for Nature cannot be fooled." Richard P. Feynman

"Technology... is a queer thing. It brings you great gifts with one hand, and it stabs you in the back with the other." C.P. Snow

"We are becoming the servants in thought, as in action, of the machine we have created to serve us." John Kenneth Galbraith

"Man is a slow, sloppy and brilliant thinker; the machine is fast, accurate, and stupid" William M. Kelly

"We live in a society exquisitely dependent on science and technology, in which hardly anyone knows anything about science and technology."
Carl Sagan

Chapter 187 Television

"Television has proved that people will look at anything rather than each other." Ann Landers

"Television is the first truly democratic culture – the first culture available to everybody and entirely governed by what people want. The most terrifying thing is what people want." Clive Barnes

"TV is chewing gum for the eyes." Frank Lloyd Wright

"I find television very educating. Every time somebody turns on a set, I go into the other room and read a book." Groucho Marx

"Television has raised writing to a new low." Samuel Goldwyn

"Television is simply automated day-dreaming." Lee Lovinger

"They say that ninety percent of TV is junk. But, ninety percent of everything is junk." Gene Roddenberry

"Television was not intended to make human beings vacuous, but it is an emanation of their vacuity." Malcolm Muggeridge

"Television's perfect. You turn a few knobs, a few of those mechanical adjustments at which the higher apes are so proficient, and lean back and drain your mind of all thought. And there you are watching the bubbles in the primeval ooze. You don't have to concentrate. You don't have to react. You don't have to remember. You don't miss your brain because you don't need it. Your heart and liver and lungs continue to function normally. Apart from that, all is peace and quiet. You are in the man's nirvana. And if the same poor nasty minded person comes along and say you look like a fly on a can of garbage, pay him no mind. He probably hasn't got the price of a television set." Raymond Chandler

"The triumph of machine over people." Fred Allen, about television

Chapter 188 Temptation

"Temptations, unlike opportunities, will always give you many second chances." Orlando A. Battista

"Most people would like to be delivered from temptation but would like it to keep in touch." Robert Orben

"Temptation rarely comes in working hours. It is in their leisure time that men are made or married." W.N. Taylor

"It is good to be without vices, but it is not good to be without temptations." Walter Bagehot

"Temptations, when we first meet them, are like a lion that roared at Samson; but if we overcome them, the next time we see them we shall find a nest of honey within them." John Bunyan

"We gain strength of the temptation we resist." Ralph Waldo Emerson

"Every moment of resistance in temptation is a victory" Frederick W. Faber

"Temptations come, as a general rule, when they are sought." Margaret Oliphant

Chapter 189 The Future

"I never think of the future – it comes soon enough." Albert Einstein

"Life wouldn't be worth living if I worried over the future as well as the present." W. Somerset Maugham

"The future ain't what it used to be." Yogi Berra

"The best thing about the future is that it only comes one day at a time." Abraham Lincoln

"The future belongs to those who believe in the beauty of their dreams." Eleanor Roosevelt

"You are the same today that you are going to be in five years from now except for two things: the people with whom you associate and the books you read." Charles Jones

"The vast possibilities of our great future will become realities only if we make ourselves responsible for that future." Gifford Pinchot

"The future is a convenient place for dreams." Anatole France

"I look to the future because that's where I'm going to spend the rest of my life." George F. Burns

Chapter 190 The Past

"Those who do cannot repeat the past are condemned to repeat it."
George Santayana

"Live neither in the past nor in the future, but let each day's work absorb your entire energies, and satisfy your widest ambition." Sir William Osler

"Stop acting as if life is a rehearsal. Live this day as if it were your last. The past is over and gone. The future is not guaranteed." Wayne Dyer

"You can clutch the past so tightly to your chest that it leaves your arms too full to embrace the present." Jan Glidewell

"I like the dreams of the future better than the history of the past." Thomas Jefferson

"I don't think the human mind can comprehend the past and the future. They are both just illusions that can manipulate you into thinking there's some kind of change" Bob Dylan

"The past is never there when you try to go back. It exists, but only in memory. To pretend otherwise is to invite a mess." Chris Cobbs

"The past may not repeat itself, but it sure does rhyme." Mark Twain

"One problem with gazing too frequently into the past is that we may turn around to find the future has run out on us." Michael Cibenko

Chapter 191 The World

"When the power of love overcomes the love of power the world will know peace." Jimi Hendrix

"Be content with what you have; rejoice in the way things are. When you realize there is nothing lacking, the whole world belongs to you." Lao Tzu

"The world is round so that friendship may encircle it." Pierre Teilhard de Chardin

"Though we travel the world over to find the beautiful, we must carry it with us or we find it not." Ralph Waldo Emerson

"The more man meditates upon good thoughts, the better will be his world and the world at large." Confucius

"This world is but a canvas to our imagination." Henry David Thoreau

"This world of ours… must avoid becoming a community of dreadful fear and hate, and be, instead, a proud conferation of mutual trust and respect." Dwight D. Eisenhower

"In wilderness is the preservation of the world." Henry David Thoreau

"Maybe this world is another planet's hell." Aldous Huxley

"Our species needs, and deserves, a citizenry with minds wide awake and basic understanding of how the world works." Carl Sagan

Chapter 192 Thought

"Our thoughts are free." Cicero

"A man is infinitely more complicated than his thoughts." Paul Valery

"In every work of genius we see our own rejected thoughts." Ralph Waldo Emerson

"Except our own thoughts, there is nothing absolutely in our power." Rene Descartes

"What we are today comes from our thoughts of yesterday, and our present thoughts build our life of tomorrow. Our life is the creation of our mind." Buddha

"Our life always expresses the result of our dominant thoughts." Soren Kierkegaard

"Thought is the parent of the deed." Thomas Carlyle

"Nurture your mind with great thoughts for you will never go any higher than you think." Benjamin Disraeli

"All that you accomplish or fail to accomplish with your life is the result of your thoughts." James Allen

"It is the power of thought that gives man power over nature." Hans Christian Anderson

Chapter 193 Time

"All that really belongs to us is time; even he who has nothing else has that." Baltasar Gracian

"Time is the coin of your life. It is the only coin you have, and only you can determine how it will be spent. Be careful lest you let other people spend it for you." Carl Sandburg

"Time is at once the most valuable and the most perishable of all our posessions." John Randolph

"Regret for wasted time is more wasted time." Mason Cooley

"Time does not change us. It just unfolds us." Max Frisch

"Time is what prevents everything from happening at once." John Archibald Wheeler

"Men talk of killing time, while time quietly kills them." Dion Boucicault

"Time is the only thief we can't get justice against." Terri Guillemets

"Time is what we want most, but ... what we use worst." William Penn

Chapter 194 Tolerance

"Nothing dies so hard, or rallies so often as intolerance." Henry Ward Beecher

"I have seen great intolerance shown in support of tolerance." Samuel Taylor Coleridge

"Intolerance is evidence of impotence" Aleister Crowley

"Travel teaches intolerance." Benjamin Disraeli

"What is objectionable, what is dangerous, about extremists is not that they are extreme, but that they are intolerant. The evil is not what they say about their cause, but what they say about their opponents." Robert Francis Kennedy

"No human trait deserves less tolerance in everyday life, and gets less, than intolerance." Giacamo Leopardi

"Since others have to tolerate my weaknesses, it is only fair that I should tolerate theirs." William Allen White

"Laws alone cannot secure freedom of expression; in order that every man presents his views without penalty there must be spirit of tolerance in the entire population." Albert Einstein

"The test of courage comes when we are in the minority. The test of tolerance comes when we are in the majority." Ralph W. Sockman

"Tolerance is giving to every other human being every right that you claim for yourself." Robert Green Ingersoll

Chapter 195 Travel

"A good traveler has no fixed plans, and is not intent on arriving." Lao Tzu

"If you reject the food, ignore the customs, fear the religion and avoid the people, you might better stay at home." James Michener

"To travel is to discover that everyone is wrong about other countries." Aldous Huxley

"All journeys have secret destinations of which the traveler is unaware." Martin Buber

"Bizarre travel plans are dancing lessons from God" Kurt Vonnegut

"The greatest reward and luxury of travel is to be able to experience everyday things as if for the first time, to be in a position in which almost nothing is so familiar it is taken for granted." Bill Bryson

"Our happiest moments as tourists always seem to come when we stumble upon one thing while in pursuit of something else." Lawrence Block

"Travel makes one modest, you see what a tiny place you occupy in the world." Gustave Flaubert

"Through travel I first became aware of the outside world; it was through travel that I found my own introspective way into becoming a a part of it." Eudora Welty

"Perhaps travel cannot prevent bigotry, but by demonstrating that all peoples cry, laugh, eat, worry, and die, it can introduce the idea that if we try and understand each other, we may even become friends." Maya Angelou

Chapter 196 Trees

"God has cared for these trees, saved them from drought, disease, avalanches, and a thousand tempests and floods. But he cannot save them from fools." John Muir

"The tree which moves some to tears of joy is in the eyes of others only a green thing that stands in the way. Some see Nature all ridicule and deformity, and some scarce see Nature at all. But to the eyes of the man of imagination. Nature is imagination itself." William Blake Steinbeck

"They kill good trees to put out bad newspapers" James G. Watt

"I frequently tramped eight or ten miles through the deepest snow to keep an appointment with a beech-tree, or a yellow birch, or an old acquaintance among the pines." Henry David Thoreau

"God is the experience of looking at a tree and saying, "Ah!"" Joseph Campbell

"I like trees because they seem more resigned to the way they have to live than other things do." Willa Cather

"Of the infinite variety of fruits which spring from the bosom of the earth, the trees of the wood are the greatest in dignity." Susan Fenimore Cooper

"The creation of a thousand forests is in one acorn." Ralph Waldo Emerson

"That each day I may walk unceasingly on the banks of my water, that my soul may repose on the branches of the trees which I planted, that I may refresh myself under the shadow of my sycamore." Egyptian tomb inscription circa 1400 BCE

"Except during the nine months before he draws his first breath, no man manages his affairs as well as a tree does." George Bernard Shaw

Chapter 197 Trust

"Mistrust the man who finds everything good, the man who finds everything evil and still more the man is indifferent to everything." Johann K. Lavater

"But the life that no longer trust another human being and no longer forms ties to the political community is not a human life any longer." Martha Nussbaum

"To be trusted is a greater compliment than being loved." George MacDonald

"Trust yourself. Create the kind of self that you will be happy to live all your life. Make the most of yourself by fanning the tiny, inner sparks of possibility into flames of achievement." Golda Meir

"You must trust and believe in people or life becomes impossible." Anton Chekhov

"No soul is desolate as long as there is a human being for whom it can feel trust and reverence." T.S Elliot

"He who believes in nobody knows that he himself is not to be trusted." Berthold Auerbach

"Someone who thinks the world is always cheating him is right. He is missing that wonderful feeling of trust in someone or something." Eric Hoffer

"No man is wise enough, nor good enough, to be trusted with unlimited power." Charles Caleb Colton

"It's a vice to trust everyone, and equally a vice to trust no one." Seneca

"It is mutual trust, even more than mutual interest that holds human associations together." H.L Mencken

Chapter 198 Truth

"All truth passes through three stages. First it is ridiculed. Second it is violently opposed. Third, it is accepted as being self-evident." Arthur Schopenhauer

"All truths are easy to understand once they are discovered; the point is to discover them." Galileo Galilei

"Rather than love, than money, than fame, give me truth." Henry David Thoreau

"Time is precious, but truth is more precious than time." Benjamin Disraeli

"We know the truth, not only by the reason, but also by the heart." Blaise Pascal

"You never find yourself until you face the truth." Pearl Bailey

"Unthinking respect for authority is the greatest enemy of the truth." Albert Einstein

"Speak your truth quietly and clearly; and listen to others, even to the dull and ignorant, they too have their story." Max Ehrman

"Truth is the property of no individual but is the treasure of all men." Ralph Waldo Emerson

"Even if you are minority of one, the truth is the truth." Mahatma Gandhi

Chapter 199 Uncertainty

"For my part I know nothing with any certainty, but the sight of the stars makes me dream." Vincent van Gogh

"Uncertainty and mystery are energies of life. Don't let them scare you unduly, for they keep boredom at bay and spark creativity." R. I. Fitzhenry

"Uncertainty will always be part of the taking charge process." Harold S. Geneen

"We sail within a vast sphere, ever drifting in uncertainty, driven from end to end." Blaise Pascal

 "Do not fight verbosity with words: speech is given to all, intelligence to few." Moralia

 "Speech is human, silence is divine, yet also brutish and dead: therefore we must learn both arts." Thomas Carlyle

 "If nobody spoke unless he had something to say, the human race would very soon lose the use of speech." W. Somerset Maugham

 "Why doesn't the fellow who says, "I'm no speechmaker," let it go at that instead of giving a demonstration?" Kin Hubbard

"Public speaking is the art of diluting a two-minute idea with a two-hour vocabulary." Evan Esar

 "Speech is power: speech is to persuade, to convert, to compel. It is to bring another out of

his bad sense into your good sense." Ralph Waldo Emerson

Chapter 200 Values

"A people that values its privileges above its principles soon loses both." Dwight D. Eisenhower

"If a nation values anything more than freedom, it will lose its freedom, and the irony of it is that if it is comfort or money that it values more, it will lose that too." W. Somerset Maugham

"So when these people sell out, even though they get fabulously rich, they're gypping themselves out of one of the potentially most rewarding experiences of their unfolding lives. Without it, they may never know their values or how to keep their newfound wealth in perspective." Steve Jobs

"A profound political question is suddenly on the table: Must the country continue to give precedence to private financial gain and market determinism over human lives and broad public values?" William Greider

"We can tell our values by looking at our checkbook stubs." Gloria Steinem

"The writer interweaves a story with his own doubts, questions, and values. That is art." Naguib Mahfouz

"Our problem is not to find better values but to be faithful to those we profess." John W. Gardner

"The true value of a human being can be found in the degree to which he has attained liberation from the self." Albert Einstein

"The longer we live the more we think and the higher the value we put on friendship and tenderness towards parents and friends." Samuel Johnson

"The good thing about being a hypocrite is that you get to keep your values." Alan Alda

Chapter 201 Vices

"Search others for their virtues, thyself for thy vices." Benjamin Franklin

"The greatest minds are capable of the greatest vices as well as of the greatest virtues." Rene Descartes

"Nothing is as certain as that the vices of leisure are gotten rid of by being busy." Seneca

"He has all the virtues I dislike and none of the vices I admire." Sir Winston Churchill

"There is more than a morsel of truth in the saying, "He who hates vice hates mankind."" W. MacNeile Dixon

"When our vices desert us, we flatter ourselves that we are deserting our vices." Francois Duc de La Rochefoucauld

"The vices of the rich and great are mistaken for error; and those of the poor and lowly, for crimes." Lady Marguerite Blessington

"The worst vice of a fanatic is his sincerity." Oscar Wilde

"I prefer an interesting vice to a virtue that bores" Moliere

"Too much work and too much energy kill a man just as effectively as too much assorted vice or too much drink" Rudyard Kipling

"Vices are often habits rather than passions" Antoine Rivarol

Chapter 202 Victory

"Force is all-conquering, but its victories are short-lived." Abraham Lincoln

"Be careful that victories do not carry the seed of future defeats." Ralph W. Sockman

"The best victory is when the opponent surrenders of its own accord before there are any actual hostilities...It is best to win without fighting." Sun-tzu

"The people who remained victorious were less like conquerors than conquered." St. Augustine

"Victory is sweetest when you've known defeat." Malcolm S. Forbes

"Victory is won not in miles but in inches. Win a little now, hold your ground, and later, win a little more." Louis L'Amour

"Once you hear the details of victory, it is hard to distinguish it from a defeat" Jean-Paul Sartre

"One of the greatest victories you can gain over someone is to beat him at politeness." Josh Billings

"There are victories of the soul and spirit. Sometimes, even if you lose, you win." Elie Wiesel

"You must not, when you have gained a victory, use any triumphing or insulting expression, nor show too much pleasure ; but endeavor to console your adversary, and make him less dissatisfied with himself by every kind and civil expression, that may be" Benjamin Franklin

"Victory and defeat are each of the same price." Thomas Jefferson

"War is a series of catastrophes that results in a victory." George Clemenceau

Chapter 203 Violence

"I object to violence because when it appears to do good, the good is only temporary; the evil it does is permanent." Mahatma Gandhi

"Much violence is based on the illusion that life is a property to be defended and not to be shared." Henri Nouwen

"The cause of violence is not ignorance. It is self-interest. Only reverance can restrain violence - reverance for human life and the environment." William Sloan Coffin

"Political history is largely an account of mass violence and of the expenditure of vast resources to cope with mythical fears and hopes" Murray Edelman

"Violence in the voice is often only the death rattle of reason in the throat." H. G. Bohn

"I give the name violence to a boldness lying idle and enamored of danger." Jean Genet

"Secrets are made to be found out with time." Charles Sanford

"The man who can keep a secret may be wise, but he is not half as wise as the man with no secrets to keep" The ultimate weakness of violence is that it is a descending spiral; returning violence with violence only multiplies voilence, adding deeper darkness to a night already devoid of stars." Martin Luther King, Jr.

"All violence is the result of people tricking themselves into believing that their pain derives from other people and that consequently those people deserve to be punished." Marshall Rosenberg
"The state calls its own violence law, but that of the individual crime."
Max Stirner

"So long as governments set the example of killing their enemies, private citizens will occasionally kill theirs." Elbert Hubbard

Chapter 204 War

"One is left with the horrible feeling now that war settles nothing; that to win a war is as disastrous as to lose one." Agatha Christie

"I know not with what weapons World War III will be fought, but World War IV will be fought with sticks and stones." Albert Einstein

"You can no more win a war than you can win an earthquake." Jeannette Rankin

"What difference does it make to the dead, the orphans and the homeless, whether the mad destruction is wrought under the name of totalitarianism or the holy name of liberty or democracy?" Mahatma Gandhi

"It is well that war is so terrible - otherwise we would grow too fond of it." Robert E. Lee

"War is a cowardly escape from the problems of peace." Thomas Mann

"All war represents a failure of diplomacy." Tony Benn

"I hate war as only a soldier who has lived it can, only as one who has seen its brutality, its stupidity." Dwight D. Eisenhower

"If you think of humanity as one large body, then war is like suicide, or at best, self mutilation." Jerome P. Crabb

Chapter 205 Wealth

"An unhurried sense of time is in itself a form of wealth." Bonnie Friedman

"It is pretty hard to tell what does bring happiness; poverty and wealth have both failed." Kin Hubbard

"Prefer loss to the wealth of dishonest gain; the former vexes you for a time; the latter will bring you lasting remorse." Chilo

"Wealth is the parent of luxury and indolence, and poverty of meanness and viciousness, and both of discontent." Plato

"Wealth is the slave of a wise man. The master of a fool." Seneca

"It is health that is real wealth and not pieces of gold and silver." Mahatma Gandhi

"It is neither wealth nor splendor; but tranquility and occupation which give you happiness." Thomas Jefferson

"The greatest wealth is to live content with little." Plato

"It is only when the rich are sick that they fully feel the impotence of wealth." Benjamin Franklin

"Honesty is the rarest wealth anyone can possess, and yet all the honesty in the world ain't lawful tender for a loaf of bread." Josh Billings

Chapter 206 Weather

"The trouble with weather forecasting is that it's right too often for us to ignore it and wrong too often for us to rely on it." Patrick Young

"Weather is a great metaphor for life — sometimes it's good, sometimes it's bad, and there's nothing much you can do about it but carry an umbrella." Terri Guillemets

"Weather forecast for tonight: dark." George Carlin

"Don't knock the weather; nine-tenths of the people couldn't start a conversation if it didn't change once in a while." Kin Hubbard

"There's no such thing as bad weather, only unsuitable clothing." Alfred Wainwright

"Change of weather is the discourse of fools." Thomas Fuller

"A change in the weather is sufficient to recreate the world and ourselves." Marcel Proust

"Some things are only capable of being done in space. Examples of that are looking at our Earth from that far away, and understanding the entire processes of storms and weather patterns, and oceans, and coastlines." Laurel Clark

"The techniques I developed for studying turbulence, like weather, also apply to the stock market." Benoit Mandelbrot

"You can have money piled to the ceiling but the size of your funeral is still going to depend on the weather." Chuck Tanner

Chapter 207 Winter

"Winter, which, being full of care, makes summer's welcome thrice more wish'd, more rare." William Shakespeare

"Sometimes our fate resembles a fruit tree in winter. Who would think that those branches would turn green again and blossom, but we hope it, we know it." Johann Wolfgang von Goethe

"Adversity draws men together and produces beauty and harmony in life's relationships, just as the cold of winter produces ice-flowers on the window-panes, which vanish with the warmth." Soren Kierkegaard

"The problem with winter sports is that - follow me closely here - they generally take place in winter." Dave Barry

"Every Winter, When the great sun has turned his face away, The earth goes down into a vale of grief, And fasts, and weeps, and shrouds herself in sables" Charles Kingsley

"Perhaps I am a bear, or some hibernating animal underneath, for the instinct to be half asleep all winter is so strong in me." Anne Morrow Lindbergh

"Winter is nature's way of saying, "Up yours."" Robert Byrne

"Winter lies too long in country towns; hangs on until it is stale and shabby, old and sullen." Willa Sibert Cather

"On the heights it is warmer than people in the valleys suppose, especially in winter. The thinker recognizes the full import of this simile." Friedrich Nietzsche

"It is a hopeless endeavour to unite the contrarieties of spring and winter; it is unjust to claim the privileges of age, and retain the play-things of childhood" Samuel Johnson

Chapter 208 Wisdom

"A wise man, recognizing that the world is but an illusion, does not act as if it is real, so he escapes the suffering." Buddha

"He that can compose himself is wiser than he that composes books." Benjamin Franklin

"The wise man will make more opportunities than he finds." Francis Bacon

"The only true wisdom is in knowing you know nothing." Socrates

"It is unwise to be too sure of one's own wisdom. It is healthy to be reminded that the strongest might weaken and the wisest might err." Mahatma Gandhi

"The strongest symptom of wisdom in man is his being sensible of his own follies." François de la Rochefoucauld

"The whole problem with the world is that fools and fanatics are always so certain of themselves, but wiser people so full of doubts." Bertrand Russell

"Wisdom comes by disillusionment." George Santayana

"Some of the best lessons we ever learn we learn from our mistakes and failures. The error of the past is the wisdom of the future." Tryon Edwards

"Wisdom outweighs any wealth." Sophocles

Chapter 209 Wishes

"Destiny has two ways of crushing us - by refusing our wishes and by fulfilling them." Henri Frederic Amiel

"When all of your wishes are granted, many of your dreams will be destroyed." Marilyn Manson

"In all professions each affects a look and an exterior to appear what he wishes the world to believe that he is. Thus we may say that the whole world is made up of appearances." Francois de La Rochefoucauld

"Great minds have purposes; others have wishes." Washington Irving

"I am indeed rich, since my income is superior to my expenses, and my expense is equal to my wishes." Edward Gibbon

"People wish to be poets more than they wish to write poetry, and that's a mistake. One should wish to celebrate more than one wishes to be celebrated." Lucille Clifton

"The problem with most people is that they think with their hopes or fears or wishes rather than their minds." Walter Duranty

"I wish they would only take me as I am." Vincent van Gogh

"Be not angry that you cannot make others as you wish them to be, since you cannot make yourself as you wish to be." Thomas Kempis

"When you're safe at home you wish you were having an adventure; when you're having an adventure you wish you were safe at home" Thornton Wilder

Chapter 210 Work

"There has never been but one question in all civilization-how to keep a few men from saying to many men: You work and earn bread and we will eat it." Abraham Lincoln

"Pleasure in the job puts perfection in the work." Aristotle

"Hard work never killed anybody, but why take a chance?" Edgar Bergen

"Get happiness out of your work or you may never know what happiness is." Elbert Hubbard

"Derive happiness in oneself from a good day's work, from illuminating the fog that surrounds us." Henri Matisse

"The only place where success comes before work is in the dictionary." Donald Kendall

"Three Rules of Work: Out of clutter find simplicity; From discord find harmony; In the middle of difficulty lies opportunity." Albert Einstein

"Work spares us from three evils: boredom, vice, and need" Voltaire

"Concentrate all your thoughts upon the work at hand. The sun's rays do not burn until brought to a focus." Alexander Graham Bell

"The sum of wisdom is that time is never lost that is devoted to work." Ralph Waldo Emerson

Chapter 211 Worries

"There is a great difference between worry and concern. A worried person sees a problem, and a concerned person solves a problem." Harold Stephens

"What worries you masters you." Haddon W. Robinson

"Worry never robs tomorrow of its sorrow, it only saps today of its joy." Leo F. Buscaglia

"Worry is a thin stream of fear trickling through the mind. If encouraged, it cuts a channel into which all other thoughts are drained." Arthur Somers Roche

"The reason why worry kills more people than work is that more people worry than work." Robert Frost

"Worry is spiritual short sight. Its cure is intelligent faith." Paul Brunton

"There are two days in the week about which and upon which I never worry... Yesterday and Tomorrow." Robert Jones Burdette

"Worry is interest paid on trouble before it comes due." W. R. Inge

"Freedom from worries and surcease from strain are illusions that always inhabit the distance." Edwin Way Teale

"If you ask what is the single most important key to longevity, I would have to say it is avoiding worry, stress and tension. And if you didn't ask me, I'd still have to say it." George F. Burns

Chapter 212 Writing

"You must stay drunk on writing so reality cannot destroy you." Ray Bradbury

"If there's a book you really want to read, but it hasn't been written yet, then you must write it." Toni Morrison

"Writing, I think, is not apart from living. Writing is a kind of double living. The writer experiences everything twice. Once in reality and once in that mirror which waits always before or behind." Catherine Drinker Bowen

"When something can be read without effort, great effort has gone into its writing." Enrique Jardiel Poncela

"Writing comes more easily if you have something to say." Sholem Asch

"The ablest writer is only a gardener first, and then a cook: his tasks are, carefully to select and cultivate his strongest and most nutritive thoughts; and when they are ripe, to dress them, wholesomely, and yet so that they may have a relish." Augustus William Hare and Julius Charles Hare

"Writing is a struggle against silence." Carlos Fuentes

"The best time for planning a book is while you're doing the dishes." Agatha Christie

"Writers are not just people who sit down and write. They hazard themselves. Every time you compose a book your composition of yourself is at stake." E.L. Doctorow

"A good style should show no signs of effort. What is written should seem a happy accident." W. Somerset Maugham

"You never have to change anything you got up in the middle of the night to write." Saul Bellow

Chapter 213 Youth

"In youth we learn; in age we understand." Marie Ebner von Eschenbach

"Youth would be an ideal state if it came a little later in life." Herbert Henry Asquith

"The youth is no longer a youth, but a man, when the first of his dreams is dead." William Herbert Carruth

"Everyone believes in his youth that the world really began with him, and that all merely exist for his sake." Johann Wolfgang Von Goethe

"There may be no fool like an old fool, but our observation has been that the young fool runs him a pretty close second." Robert Elliot Gonzales

"The young are permanently in a state resembling intoxication." Aristotle

"Except for an occasional heart attack I feel as young as I ever did." Robert Benchley

"Time misspent in youth is sometimes all the freedom one ever has." Anita Brookner

"What Youth deemed crystal, Age finds out was dew." Robert Browning

"The Youth of a Nation are the trustees of posterity." Benjamin Disraeli

Conclusions

Thank you for sharing this journey through my favorite quotes. All of them have a special meaning for me, and I hope they provoked some reflection for you. I am going to continue to produce multiple volumes of my favorites in a series of books with different topics. I hope you enjoyed this collection. If you prefer shorter books with subsets of the topics covered in this book, please check out the individual volumes in this series (volumes 1 to 18 of My Favourite Quotes) in the Kindle Store.

Made in USA - North Chelmsford, MA
85481_9781701376083
03.12.2024 2116